D1488780

Discipleship and Its Foundations

A Jesuit Retreat

David L. Fleming SJ

Review for Religious
St. Louis, Missouri
2005

Acknowledgments

Cover: Ignatius Loyola, pilgrim and penitent, an oil painting by Ms. Montserrat Gudiol (1991), in the Holy Cave, Manresa, Spain.

IHS images: from Ars Jesuitica CD, The Institute of Jesuit Sources, 2000, except for page 9, which is from the photos of Rev. John T. Quinn SJ.

Review for Religious
3601 Lindell Boulevard
St. Louis, Missouri 63108

ISBN 0-924768-13-4

Contents

Preface

I was privileged to be invited to conduct the Jesuit California Province retreat in August 2004. This book captures the basic presentation that I gave at that time, with the addition of the chapter on "The Standards." Even though I have allowed the presentations to remain as they were made to a Jesuit retreatant group, I hope that the sometimes male and Jesuit references will not prevent others from using this book for prayerful reading or their own retreat.

Because of the original Jesuit audience, I presume a certain familiarity with the *Spiritual Exercises of St. Ignatius*. I hope that the many others who have a similar familiarity will feel similarly at home. The text of the *Exercises*, then, is a suggested accompaniment to this book.

At the beginning of each presentation, I led the group in a special prayer for the grace of that particular day. I also handed out a brief set of points for the prayer periods of the day. In this written form, I have included the prayer preceding the presentation, and, after the presentation, the set of points and a repetition of the prayer to reemphasize the grace we desire.

For all who read and hopefully pray the contents of this book, I hope that these practical prayer exercises may help toward a more deeply felt appreciation of the Ignatian Exercises that I have presented in other, more conceptual books.

I am grateful to my Jesuit companions and our colleagues with whom I have worked, particularly in this Jesuit retreat. May the graces that have been special to these retreatants and their directors overflow to all who now enter into this presentation of these prayer exercises.

David L. Fleming SJ

Introduction to Our Retreat

Ignatian spirituality is unique in the church because it finds its foundation in an exercise book. One cannot call his or her spirituality Ignatian without some familiarity with the Spiritual Exercises of St. Ignatius. So for us Jesuits I think that I am safe in presuming our exposure to the Exercises book of Ignatius. But an exercise book is not written to be read, but to be worked with. We might say, then, that Ignatian spirituality is always a work in progress—which should tell you that we Jesuits, too, are always a work in progress. Since our knowledge of the Exercises will differ among us—perhaps for some either because of a relatively brief time in the Society or due to a long history of making retreats or others because of serious study of the Exercises or its lack and still for others a lot of retreat giving or almost none—I will try to do my best to explain my Ignatian references and their meaning simply.

Again, another reflection about keeping us all together. How do we define or describe spirituality? For me, a spirituality is about relationships. A spirituality is a way of relating to God, relating to myself, relating to others, and relating to my world—for us Christians—in the light of Jesus Christ, the Gospels, and the church. Ignatian spirituality is a particular Christian spirituality seen through the prisms of Ignatius Loyola's gifts and graces shared with the church and the Society of Jesus he founded.

For the most part, in a retreat we are dealing more often with spiritual practice—our inner work—rather than with a study or theory of spirituality. But I will confess that in these retreat conferences we may seem to be weaving back and forth between a kind of study of Ignatian spirituality through our reflections on certain exercises and our practical (praying) experience of it.

After these preliminaries, I want to add a prenote. My prenote deals with the emphasis I have given to these retreat presentations: my stressing that these are exercises for the heart. We likely are familiar that Ignatius begins his book with twenty notes or, as he calls them, annotations. His very first note draws our attention to the comparison of physical and spiritual exercises. Just as there are various exercises we identify as physical, so there are exercises that we call spiritual. Just as there are many kinds of physical exercises, so, too, there are many kinds of spiritual exercises.

I would like to suggest that we might further refine the Ignatian reference to spiritual exercises to "exercises for the heart." Heart, in ancient biblical usage and even in our contemporary American usage, describes persons in their total response to other persons or events. Examples: "My heart goes out to you." "This situation speaks to my heart." *Heart* takes in my mind, my feelings, my body, and my soul.

When I speak of "exercises for the heart," I indicate that I believe Ignatius is not talking about spiritual exercises meaning only exercises of the mind or the will, but particularly he wants to exercise the heart. He wants us to have long ears, like a rabbit, so that we can listen to our heart. That is what happened to him. And yet sometimes the commentators on the Exercises and, perhaps, we ourselves (often because of the way we were directed in a retreat) are trying to focus on a conversion of mind or of will, trying to change how we think or what we do. Ignatius would be concerned more about the heart. And I believe that if we look particularly at certain structural exercises of the Spiritual Exercises, we will discover a new richness if we consciously emphasize the heart.

Now let me say what I hope that we might together pray for in this retreat. Back in June 2002, the Vatican Congregation for Institutes of Consecrated Life and Societies of Apostolic Life issued an instruction with the captivating title of "Starting Afresh from Christ." This document alerted us that we as religious (let me say, as Jesuits) cannot be creative, capable of renewing ourselves and our communities, and opening new pastoral paths, if we do not feel loved by Christ. It is this felt love that makes us strong and courageous, that instills fire, and enables us to be daring in all that we do. This is where we always hope to be each day: starting afresh from Christ. In our Jesuit lives—from early on, sometimes perhaps as shortly as after the 30-day novitiate retreat, and as late as celebrating 50 years as a Jesuit priest or brother—we can find ourselves with a need to "start afresh from Christ."

As you might expect, then, the focus of this retreat is Jesus, and more precisely our growth in relationship to Jesus, maybe with a feel or with the reality of "starting afresh." I am struck that in the Second Week of the Exercises Ignatius suggests that we consistently pray for one central grace. We pray to know Jesus more intimately. Sometimes we hear the English translation of praying for an "interior knowledge," but I think that our English word *intimate* better captures Ignatius's intent. We want to be given the grace of an *intimacy with Jesus*.

Everything else about our lives flows from such an intimacy. As an intimate relationship develops, we certainly will love him more, and then it follows that we will be able to follow him more closely. Of course, in addition, it is always because we have an intimacy with Jesus that we are enabled to discern. For Ignatian discernment, as we well know, is not about the head decision, but about the heart decision. So, as I will repeat each day, the general prayer intention that I am suggesting is that we pray for the grace of an intimate relationship with Jesus. Of course, you with your director may specify or restate the grace you need to pray for in this retreat. But, for me, "I want to know Jesus" is our prayer in this retreat, just as it was the plea of St. Paul's prayer.

Creation Prayer

God, our Creator and Lord, we ask you for that gift you promised through your prophets. As we enter into this retreat, remove from us our stony hearts. Create in us fleshy hearts, hearts like your own.

Help us to see with the eyes of our heart. Help us to hear with the ears of our heart. Then we will be able to thank you for seeing all of your creation in you. We will rejoice in hearing your voice through the people and events you make present in our world.

May your kingdom come. We ask this in Jesus' name.

10

Creation

In this first presentation, I want to set the context for what I will describe as the visions of St. Ignatius as we see them in the *Spiritual Exercises*. What I am calling "visions," Ignatius, for examples, identifies as the Principle and Foundation at the very beginning of the Exercises, the Call of the King which apparently begins the Second Week, and the Contemplation on the Love of God which concludes the whole Exercises prayer time. I believe that the visions that Ignatius shares with us in these various Weeks of the Exercises derive from the "lessons" that God taught him during his own "retreat" time in Manresa.

Ignatius himself did not use the word *lesson* when he spoke of what he saw when he relates his Manresan experiences in his *Autobiography* [28-30]. Instead he used the same word as he will use in breaking down the Gospel incident for prayer; he will use the word *punto*. *Punto* (translated as *point*) indicates such a density of reflective experience that unless we take time with it we will miss the richness contained within. Ignatius had referred to God as his schoolmaster and himself the learner during the time at Manresa when he did the first note-taking which eventually resulted in his book *Spiritual Exercises*. It is interesting that Ignatius uses the word *puntos* for the "lessons" that he was taught. He applies the same word when he wants to be helpful to the retreatant for getting inside or making one's own the meditation or contemplation material.

What is the first lesson that God seemed to teach Ignatius? The first lesson that Ignatius was taught at Manresa is all about vision. Ignatius's "visions" are not something to be seen. It is not like the visions of our Lady at Lourdes had by Bernadette or the visions of Our Lord of Divine Mercy had by St. Faustina. For Ignatius, vision is an "aha" experience, but even more than just gaining an insight. Vision is an exercise of the heart. Unless our hearts are enlarged by exercises, we will remain narrow and constricted and fixed on self. Vision, then, is not just a matter of seeing. We can look and look and really not see. We can come to an understanding of a great number of things, but it may not affect our living. The Ignatian emphasis on vision is an exercising of the heart because that is what happened to him. It is the reason why, thirty years after the original experience at Manresa, Ignatius can relate to us his visions, lessons taught by God, in his *Autobiography*. It is the whole of our person involved in the very act of visioning.

Let us look at the first exercise of the Exercises titled the Principle and Foundation. From the time of the restoration of the Society of Jesus in 1814 up through the 1960s, the primary interpretation of this exercise was that of a philosophical or intellectual approach. The exercise appealed to reason. Let me first of all say that from evidence it seems that Ignatius more likely included this reflective piece while he was in his university studies at Paris. So does the statement have an intellectual component? It would be foolish to deny it. But is it primarily meant to appeal to rational thought? I do not think so. I believe that this is the first example of what I call an "exercise of the heart."

Ignatius is not just presenting an account of creation. He is seeing, because of God's teaching him. We need to view the Principle and Foundation in the context of Ignatius's Manresan visions or lessons. The first vision is about God. Ignatius experienced God the Trinity as a musical sound of three organ keys. There was beauty, there was unity, there was communion. It paradoxically is a "hearing" vision. It happened only once—a huge consolation for Ignatius. With such unity and communion, God is Love. And the second vision is about creation. Something white with rays coming out from it. But the rays always remain in relationship to the white source. Creation is a flow of God's gifting, with a human response being the link that allows the flow to return to God. But the human response must be a choice, among the goods of God's creation, for the ones that allow a person to come to know and love God and want to live with God forever. Being the limited human beings that we are, we cannot have it all. Life is choice, our choice among all the gifting of God, which this world represents. Even more directly, as the good retreat director knows, in the first colloquy of the first exercise on sin in the First Week—the colloquy being the intimate conversation time in prayer—Ignatius carefully identifies Christ as Creator, even as he hangs on the cross in front of us. This is the Pauline Christ of Colossians and Ephesians; it is the Johannine Christ identified as the Word in the Prologue of John's Gospel, the Word "in whom all things are created." And so, for Ignatius, the God of the Principle and Foundation is not seen as an abstract philosophical God, not a rational God, but a God seen in the face of Jesus Christ, Son of God, Word of God, the Alpha and the Omega of John's Apocalypse. Our hearts are taking in

13

a God of gifting, a gifting of superabundance, a superabundance of gifts that demands choices on our part to respond, to give thanks, to come to know and love this God ever better. That is a picture of our world; it is a picture of what life is all about. The Principle and Foundation simply exercises us about our own question: what is life all about? We are being given a vision that only a heart can respond to.

We find Ignatius emphasizing that we can see not only a God who loves us into existence (that is, gifts us with creation), but also One who continues to give gifts— in fact, surrounds us with gifts so that we might come to know and love and respond to this God. All of these gifts talk to us about God; God is communicating with us through all his gifts. In fact, as Ignatius sees creation as gift, it can only be seen "in God"—not God and something alongside, that is, the gifts of creation. The gifts of creation are like rays of light that have their reality only when seen in their source, light itself, or, as we say, "in God." The question in creation posed to us is: How do we listen and how do we respond? We can see a God who bids us to choose from among the gifts given us according to how much these gifts help us "to seek and to find" God, to deepen our relationship with God. For, in Ignatius's vision, all these gifts are found "in God." *That* is one way of summarizing the Ignatian Principle and Foundation.

Only One God

We might note that Ignatius does not use the word *love* in the text of the Principle and Foundation. What is more important, however, is the fact that *we* bring (just as Ignatius did) to the Ignatian paragraph our biblical notion of a God of love. Since we know that Ignatius has a closing prayer exercise titled "Contemplation on the

Love of God," we are aware that the continuity of the face of God from the beginning of the Ignatian Exercises until the end is that of a loving God. The director of the retreat is not presenting two conflicting Gods—one who is indifferent and withdrawn and one who is involved and loving. As retreatants we do not approach the Principle and Foundation with a blank, inquiring, philosophical mind. We bring our faith and our experience of God, especially in Jesus Christ. God creates and God's very being is communion.

As the Australian Jesuit Scripture scholar Anthony Campbell stresses in his book *God First Loved Us*, some contemporary translations of Scripture can be deficient in the clarity of the translation and lead us astray. As a matter of fact we do not find in Scripture God saying, "*If* you do such and such, I will love you." God does not say: "I will love you *only if* you kill your firstborn; I will love you *only if* you go to Lourdes; or I will love you *only if* you keep my commandments." God is always Love loving or a Giver gifting. *That* truly is the image that Ignatius is checking to see if we are feeling at home with as we enter into a retreat. *That* is our foundational image of God.

Because we believe in a God of love, "unconditional love," *therefore* it follows that the choices that we make in life are, deep down, all about our seeking and finding the Giver of these gifts which reflect him. If some gifts seem to lead us away from God, no matter how good the gift, we decide that these gifts are not helpful to us and so we turn away from them. Ignatius seems to indicate that our behavior follows upon our *realizing* that God loves us into existence and seeks our cooperation in our growth and fullness of life. God loves us from the beginning, with no conditions imposed on us. Knowing that we are God's beloved, we desire to behave and act in ways like God, the one who loves us into existence. There is a great

15

difference between seeing the face of a God who loves us *only on condition* that we do or act in such a way and seeing the face of a God who loves us unconditionally and *as a consequence* we want to act—to respond—in a loving way.

When we truly drink in deeply that God loves us now, as we are, then we realize that our life is not a time of testing. Lovers do not test. Our life is a time of growing and maturing. As St. Paul describes it, it goes from using a baby formula to eventually eating solid food—maturing in Christ. We are growing in our responsibility to make choices as God's loved ones. This is what Jesus preached and taught. It is the Good News. This is what Ignatius continues to share with us in the Principle and Foundation.

Love's Environment

When we live in God's unconditional love, this world is hardly a valley of tears. Rather we see it as a world of God's gifting. But God's loved creation does cry out for us to act with God to bring it to a fulfillment and so to bring about the "kingdom of God," a reign of justice and love. This, too, is what Jesus preached and taught. God entered into his creation in a definitive way in Jesus Christ—as Ignatius helps us to realize. With the defining life, death, and resurrection of Jesus, God has entered all of us into the assured victorious struggle against every limiting factor, physical, psychological, and spiritual.

Now, with the Principle and Foundation as our vision context, a context of a loving God gifting and waiting for our response, I want to suggest a few passages from the New Testament that might lead us on further into our prayer, with our grace request of coming to know Jesus more intimately. Although Ignatius in the Principle and Foundation statement avoids saying that people are gifts in order not to reduce them to being gifts for some selfish purpose of ours, there is still a way of seeing people that God has put into our lives as most precious gifts—as we are gifts for them. In this light, Jesus is God's greatest gift to us, and how we respond to Jesus is implied in the Principle and Foundation. Besides, Jesus himself continues to offer us his gifts—a most precious one is his continuing call to each of us. So that is our context of these New Testament passages for our personal prayer time.

The first passage I suggest is John 1:35-42. It is a passage about John pointing out to his disciples, "There is the Lamb of God." The two disciples follow after Jesus; he turns and seeing them following asks, "What are you looking for?" And they say, "Where do you stay?" Now *stay, remain, dwell, pitch a tent*, are significant words in John's Gospel. Jesus is One who wants to pitch his tent, stay, remain with us. And so Jesus says, "Come and see" to these two disciples. There is a seeing—what vision are they given? For they *stayed*, so the Scriptures tell us. And then follows the story of Andrew's sharing of the call with Simon. A gifting through a gifting received, first Andrew receives and then *through* Andrew comes the gifting of Jesus to Simon Peter.

A second passage I suggest follows immediately upon this one in John. It is John 1:43-51. It is the story of the call and gifting to Nathaniel (Bartholomew). Again we have talk of a seeing or visioning. Contemplate or rest in the scene. Then, perhaps, in our conversation—our colloquy—we might ask ourselves: What are the moments in our vocational call that like Nathaniel *we* are impressed by—and what is it that *Jesus* wants us to be impressed by? Are we listening and are we seeing? If you want, there is a third passage that might be helpful to your prayer: Mark 10:46-52, the well-known passage about the blind Bartimaeus. Bartimaeus, to Jesus' question "What do you

17

want me to do for you?" cries out "I want to see." But what does this gift mean for his future? He can no longer beg, like a blind man. He can no longer impose on others with his needs. He can no longer live the way he has been accustomed to live. In our contemplation, resting with Bartimaeus and with Jesus, perhaps in our colloquy we too might reflect on how asking to see is asking for a total change in the way we live in relationship to Jesus (God), and to others, and to our world.

We are asking for something from the heart. To respond, it takes people of greatheartedness (Ignatius in Annotation [5] calls it magnanimity), a necessary quality of a retreatant. We need God's grace. Because Jesus invites us, we ask for an intimacy with Jesus.

Creation

Review Outline

- Throughout the Exercises Ignatius is concerned with the movement in our hearts.

- We are always starting afresh from Christ, a theme of this retreat.

- Consistent grace we pray for: a more intimate relationship with Jesus.

- Our context is the Ignatian Principle and Foundation (SpEx 23).

- We bring love to our understanding of the God of the Principle and Foundation.

- Who is this God? a God of unconditional Love.

- Gospel passages for prayer:
    John 1:35-42, Jesus and two disciples and Simon Peter
    John 1:43-51, Jesus and Nathaniel
    Mark 10:46-52, Jesus and Bartimaeus

— ⟨✦⟩ —

Creation Prayer

God, our Creator and Lord, we ask you for that gift you promised through your prophets. As we enter into this retreat, remove from us our stony hearts. Create in us fleshy hearts, hearts like your own.

Help us to see with the eyes of our heart. Help us to hear with the ears of our heart. Then we will be able to thank you for seeing all of your creation in you. We will rejoice in hearing your voice through the people and events you make present in our world.

May your kingdom come. We ask this in Jesus' name.

Sin-and-the-Cross Prayer

God our Father, we thank you for this special time that we have to spend with you. We ask for an ever greater portion of your Spirit so that you see in us what you see in your Son Jesus.

We are sorry for the ways we have not lived as your sons, squandering the inheritance you have shared with us. It is true that we are not worthy to be called your sons. But see us now in the Company of Jesus. He has called us to be his companions.

Held in his embrace, may we rest in your merciful love. This is our prayer, in Jesus' name.

Sin and the Cross

In his second letter to the church at Corinth, we can imagine that St. Paul is only echoing the words of Jesus to us: "I have spoken to you frankly, opening my heart wide to you. There is no lack of room for you in me. The narrowness of heart is in you. Open wide your hearts."

It seems to me that Ignatius gives us exercises that are aimed at opening our hearts, enlarging our hearts; exercises that put us in shape, give our hearts good muscle fitness. We seek to be united with God not just in the religious context of prayer but also in the complexities of everyday life. That requires a healthy heart in each one of us.

In the second annotation at the beginning of the Exercises book, Ignatius cautions the director or the one who is giving the exercises not to let the *matter* or a *thought* or the *insight* capture the attention and win the first place within the retreatant's prayer. Rather the "savoring" or the "relishing" that comes from God's dealing directly with the individual is to be prized. Again I believe that Ignatius is calling our attention to the fact that he intends the emphasis to be on the exercises for the heart.

The Principle and Foundation is the first exercise of the Ignatian retreat. Its very title bluntly states its place in the Exercises. Ignatius wants to ensure that the director and the retreatant agree on a basic *ground*work of faith—to use the "foundation" image—on which the retreat can build or from which it can move upward. Yesterday we looked at this foundation exercise, especially focusing our vision on the face of Jesus as we encountered him in our prayer. Our big vision—a gifting God or Love loving—took on concrete reality from our small visions of looking at our relationship with Jesus in certain Gospel passages.

Today I am proposing that we can find Ignatius developing a kind of foundation exercise proper to each Week. In fact, as I see our call to discipleship, this call rests on and is build up not only on certain visions, but also on a number of foundations found throughout the Exercises. As we continue to pray for a growing intimacy with Jesus, I would like to continue to explore with you some of these Ignatian foundations, not as the *focus* but as the *context* of our prayer. It is my hope that familiar Gospel passages take on a new richness of insight and meaning because of the context in which they are viewed. Today I want to turn our attention to the first exercise of the First Week and begin to see or envision it as a foundational exercise—obviously first for that Week of the Exercises, but more broadly for the living of Ignatian spirituality from the heart.

Let me remind you that we cannot expect to move through the dynamics and graces of all four Weeks of the Exercises in a shorter annual retreat such as this. I am using certain structure or foundational exercises to provide a *context* or an *horizon* for the single focused grace I am suggesting for this retreat: a more intimate relationship with Jesus. That is the reason I keep emphasizing that the exercises of Ignatius, by his own intention, focus on the heart.

Ignatius presents the first exercise of the First Week as a meditation on sin, sin objectively considered. We examine the one sin of the angels, the original sin of Adam and Eve, and the single sin of a person rejecting God forever. Ignatius intends for us to come to an appreciation of the awfulness of sin, not from the weight of numbers or from its pervasiveness, but from its very nature in a single act. We note that he does not have us pray for an *understanding* of sin since sin remains a central part of the *mystery* of evil. But Ignatius directs that we pray for the grace of shame and confusion, which we might suspect at first glance to be Ignatius's effort to have us feel bad and become introspective and self-focused. Yet since we are looking at the sin of others (our own sinful actions will be reviewed in the second exercise of the First Week), our response is not subjectively motivated. And we are asking for a grace, a gift—not something we do to ourselves, like feel guilty. Often we do not wait for the gift to be given. We whomp up our own guilty feelings and induce our own shame. It has little to do with relationship, relationship with God, and is rather all self-focused. How does Ignatius approach it? By suggesting an imaginative approach to the colloquy— picturing ourselves present to Jesus, our Creator, as he hangs upon the cross—Ignatius sets the scene for our conversation, the conversation between Jesus and ourselves. The questions that Ignatius proposes—What have I done for Christ? What am I doing for Christ? What ought I to do for Christ?—are not accusatory questions, demanding a confession-like response. Rather, the grace we seek (the second prelude, which is asking for the grace of shame and confusion) and our conversation with Christ on the cross (the colloquy) fit together as a coherent unit. Before we pose these questions to ourselves, we wonder with Christ how he, being Creator of all, enjoying eternal life, has come to this end, for us sinners.

As we enter into conversation with Jesus on the cross, we are seeing and hearing and feeling Jesus' response to the sin and evil before him. In his love for us, which by our faith we have learned is what truly nails him to the cross, he is the first to feel ashamed of our human behavior and he is the one who is left confused by hatred and rejection of his love. In our conversation, Jesus shares with us this grace of shame and confusion. We are being gifted to see and respond to evil and sin the way God sees and responds to evil and sin. The foundation exercise of the First Week does not focus on *our* response to sin, but rather lets us enter into God's response to sin. This exercise, then, situates us with God, and God graces us with Christ's response to sin, which then we pray that it will be our stance towards sin, that we are entering into the Christ (and Christ-ian) response to sin.

Entering into Jesus' response to sin reminds me of the prophet Jeremiah's story about the loincloth. For Jeremiah, God is a very down-to-earth person who wants to describe the closeness he feels to us human beings by the imagery that we are like his underwear. There is an intimacy about our relationship with God. The problem with underwear is that it can get soiled or torn or worn out. Like a mother who wants us always to have clean underwear in case we get into an accident and are taken to a hospital (otherwise she will be so ashamed), so God can be ashamed of this underwear that he calls his when it is such a mess. The story provokes us to ask: What kind of underwear for God are we? In a similar way to the imagery of Jeremiah, we have Jesus sharing with us his own experience of being human— just like us in all things but sin. For *that* (sinfulness) in us, he feels shame (for us) and confusion (what did he do to us?)— and he invites us into his feelings.

Shame and confusion are relational words. Shame and confusion are not *in* us (much less *are* we shame and confusion, just as we *are* not sin, but we can commit sin). Remember St. Paul's provocative expression that "God made [Jesus] to be sin" (2 Cor 5)—for our sake, something we could never be. But there is, for us, shame and confusion because of the spoiled relationship with Jesus (God), again because of what we can do.

Now that Jesus has allowed us to share his response, we can then look at our own history of sin and evil. The grace of shame and confusion assumes a new shape as a grace of our personal sorrow and, perhaps, even tears from recognizing our part in the continuing rejection of the One who continues to love us and shower us with gifts. The rest of this first day, as well the rest of the Week, flows from the spring-source of this first exercise (why it too is truly a *principle* [source] as well as foundation-like exercise). When we enter the First Week through the door of its own foundational exercise, then the introspective, breast-beating kind of behavior that is sometimes associated with the "Week on sin" is less likely to become our focus. Surely the feelings of sadness, the sense of being in darkness, and the weight of the petty meanness of our life are part of personal responses that naturally fill out the shame-and-confusion grace. But throughout the Week constantly Ignatius keeps our eyes on God and Jesus. We find ourselves continually saying "thanks" to a God who ever loves and gifts and forgives—a God of unconditional love. Even in the face of a hell that the weight of sin impresses upon us—the fifth and final exercise of the Ignatian first day—we still look, by Ignatius's own directions, only with gratitude to Jesus as our saving and forgiving God.

Our ability to accept the awfulness of sin is a response to God, and the place of sin in our own life is measured by our acceptance of God unconditionally loving us. No wonder that the prodigal son parable captures our heart so profoundly.

Hopefully this First Week foundation caught up in the colloquy with Jesus on the Cross will provide a context for our praying of some Gospel passages today. My first suggestion is Luke 5:1-11, a passage that makes present to

25

us the call of the first disciples. Again notice how Jesus is always gifting. Note, too, that Peter's response may seem to relate us to this First Week foundation. As we are being drawn closer by Jesus, we may enter into Peter's protest of "Go away" or "I can't do it." And then we need to listen to Jesus. As an aside, I might note that in the Gospels Jesus calls people (his apostles) first (as in the Ignatian Call of the King) and it seems that only later (e.g., Peter in his denials) will they go through a First Week experience.

The second passage I suggest is Luke 5:27-32, the call of Levi (Matthew). We note again how Jesus is the initiator, and Levi is the respondent. How can someone like Levi be so immediate in his response? Does Jesus help us find an answer to this very question of ours? Rest in their relationship and then let the conversation, the colloquy, take you where it will.

Another possible passage is Luke 7:36-50, the passage about the penitent woman at the Pharisee Simon's house. The situation would certainly seem to be uncomfortable for all the dinner guests, perhaps even a bit scandalous—that is, all the guests but Jesus. Again note how Jesus invites Simon to a change in his perspective—and perhaps the guests too. Pay attention to how Jesus identifies the woman's faith and her love—two aspects of her relationship with Jesus. Why can we call Jesus our Savior? Because our own admission of sin in our life serves only to deepen our relationship with Jesus. Like Jesus reaching out his hand *immediately* to Peter as he cries out when he is sinking in the sea, so we find ourselves crying out "Lord, save me."

Remember that we continue to pray for the grace to grow in an intimate relationship with Jesus. Of course, each one of us can make that grace more specific according to how God is moving in us (perhaps with the help of our director).

Sin and the Cross

Review Outline

– Ignatius seems to have a number of "foundations" through the Weeks of the Exercises. These foundations are important for giving us the context of our prayer.

– Ignatian emphasis is always on the response of the heart.

– The grace we pray for is a more intimate relationship with Jesus.

– The First Exercise of the First Week (SpEx 45-53) is foundational. The colloquy with Christ on the cross is key, seen in relation to the grace of the exercise.

– Jesus enters us into his grace.

– Gospel passages for prayer:
  Luke 5:1-11, Jesus and Peter
  Luke 5:27-32, Jesus and Matthew
  Luke 7:36-50, Jesus, Simon, and the penitent woman

— ༼ঔৣ৪৹ —

Sin-and-the-Cross Prayer

God our Father, we thank you for this special time that we have to spend with you. We ask for an ever greater portion of your Spirit so that you see in us what you see in your Son Jesus.

We are sorry for the ways we have not lived as your sons, squandering the inheritance you have shared with us. It is true that we are not worthy to be called your sons. But see us now in the Company of Jesus. He has called us to be his companions.

Held in his embrace, may we rest in your merciful love. This is our prayer, in Jesus' name.

27

Call Prayer

God our Father, on the occasion of the transfiguration, you asked us to listen to your Son. Obedient to your call, we are trying to follow your Son's lead in our lives.

We thank you for calling us into the Society that bears your Son's name. We ask pardon for the times that we have no longer listened, but went on our own way. We failed to follow. We have obscured our identity of being his companions.

Grant us now a heart renewed. Let us start afresh in listening to how Jesus is calling to us now. Increase in us our desires to live more closely with him as his companions. We ask this in his name.

The Call of Christ

In Ignatian spirituality, our following of Jesus is based on a number of vision exercises and foundation exercises.

The exercise Call of the King has traditionally been identified as foundational, not only to the Second Week, but to the following Weeks, all of which focus on Christ. Ignatius has identified this exercise as a "help" toward contemplating the life of Christ. What is striking about the exercise is the objective approach that Ignatius employs. Not only does he begin with the parable-story of a king and his call, but he also makes the comparison to the risen Christ, who is even now calling out to everyone to be his follower. In the second prelude of the exercise, we are asking for the grace not to be deaf to Christ's call—to be ready and eager to do what he desires. The seeking of grace is the only subjective aspect of the exercise. While in most exercises of the retreat the director assesses the movement of the particular exercise by listening carefully to what grace the retreatant prays for in the prelude, and then to what in the conversation or colloquy time the retreatant and God talk about, here in the Call of the King exercise there is only the prelude, and no colloquy is suggested. Instead of the subjective interactive response that makes up the colloquy, Ignatius would have us listen to the objective response of the magnanimous and generous person. We find ourselves inspired, we are being given a good model, and we hear the prayer of the person on fire to serve. As retreatants we are truly disciples, "student-learners," and so we may not be able at this time to speak out meaningfully such a generous spiritual response as we hear from others in this third point [98]. But Ignatius has planted the seed (and we have asked for that grace), and now we want to observe Jesus carefully so that we may come to really know him and drink in all that it means for us to make our response by following him. In this way the Call of the King exercise is the spring-source exercise (I repeat that using the expression *spring-source* emphasizes that this exercise is truly a *principle* (a source as well as a foundation) from which flows our wanting to know Christ Jesus in the exercises of the Second Week that follow.

While the Call of the King exercise does look forward to the rest of the Week, it also has a way of looking back toward the First Week. Jesus invites us all, in a way that is very particular and unique to each person, to have a part in his saving mission. If we felt ourselves the recipients of Jesus' saving action in the First Week, now we hear ourselves invited to "be with" Jesus and to "work with" Jesus. Jesus wants us to play an integral role with him in the saving action of God. This exercise, then, finishes the First Week as a true expression of God's mercy. God is not content with doing something *for* us, but seeks *to involve us* in his merciful action. God's mercy is experienced in his desire to have us work with him in bringing about the kingdom.

We are changing our imagery (from the foundation idea) when we describe the Call of the King exercise as a "bridge" prayer period between the First Week and the Second Week. It can truly be said to complete the First Week inasmuch as Christ's seeking us out and calling to us is reminiscent of the father running out to greet his prodigal son in Jesus' parable. The call to be Christ's disciple incarnates God's mercy. We resonate with Peter's response to Christ's call: "Leave me, Lord, for I am a sinful man" (Lk 5:8). When we consider the same prayer exercise as directing us towards the Second Week, it leads us perhaps even more obviously to pray the gospel mysteries with the clear intention of coming to know God as the One who is calling and who seeks our love and following.

We remember that Ignatius had two books to read during his convalescent time at Loyola castle. The first book, the life of Christ as told in Ludolph's conflation of Gospels, emphasizing the words and deeds of Jesus, and the second book, the lives of the saints as collected and picturesquely narrated by Voragine, fed Ignatius's imagination even better than the romance novels that he had asked for. In fact, he started noting or observing that in his daydreams and imaginings about his life during his convalescent period at Loyola something different was happening inside him. He would dream about his life as a hero in terms of his service of his Spanish king, and after his initial excitement he was left with an unsatisfied or empty feeling. But when he imaged himself on the models of the saints in following Jesus, in serving God, then he was surprised that the feelings stayed with him of enthusiasm and joy and satisfaction. Ignatius identifies this period as the beginning of his understanding of a process of "discerning" how God works with us.

Whatever led Iñigo Loyola to change his name to Ignatius, we are not sure. But we can be sure that it was imaginative because Ignatius is a very imaginative man.

Using imagination is important for entering into his Exercises. For Ignatius, to contemplate is an imaginative exercise. Contemplation has been a longtime component of Christian spirituality in ways similar to its being an integral part of other religious traditions. Usually contemplation refers to a "gazing at" or a "resting in" the divine. Our contemporary emphasis on centering prayer is a form of

31

this kind of traditional use of the prayer form of contemplation. But, when Ignatius asks us to contemplate, he is pointing us to use all our imaginative powers to enter as fully as we can into the incidents (or "mysteries" as we call them) of the Gospels.

Ignatius proposes two ways of entering into contemplation. First in the incarnation/annunciation mystery, which is the first contemplation of the Second Week, Ignatius suggests that we can enter into contemplation by our taking our stance with God and being as fully involved as God is in this mystery, as he is in each of the mysteries we consider. The second way, which Ignatius briefly describes as he points the mystery of the nativity of Jesus, involves our total presence within the Gospel incident. We are to look at what we see, we are to listen to what we hear, we are to observe with a keen and sensitive heart all that goes on. Ignatius suggests that we might even insert ourselves as a participant within the Gospel mystery, so truly are we present.

A number of people often indicate that this kind of contemplation is not their gift. They are just not very imaginative. Perhaps TV and video screens have dulled their own creative powers. Maybe they are just more of a scientific, factual bent. However that might be, I believe that I would just ask if they had ever told a story. I expect them to agree that they have told stories about their own experiences or others'. All we need is the leading question: "How has your day been?" Then we begin telling stories. In order to enter into Ignatian contemplation, I would suggest that they might just tell the Gospel story to themselves. When they tell the story, what do they see, what do they hear, what takes place? I think that many people might find entering into Ignatian contemplation easier than they thought if they just remember how they tell a story.

Our dreams—not our nighttime sleep ones, but our daydreams, our imaginings of the shape of our ideals, our hopes, our successes—are empowered by our imagination. The way that the early church communities remembered Jesus and set down the Gospels depicts Jesus as a creative, imaginative man. Jesus shares his dreams with us in his Sermon on the Mount—the kind of dreaming that Ignatius picks up on to picture Christ and his call to all of us in his Second Week meditation on the Call of the King. All the parables that Jesus tells, all the symbolic actions he performs in feeding the multitudes, in healing the blind, and in curing the deaf involve the use of imagination. In fostering the use of our imagination in prayer, it is as if Ignatius is having us use this gift of God to find God, to enter into imagination which identifies our creator God and the action of God and so also allows us to identify ourselves with his Son Jesus.

Entering into the Gospel story through the use of our imagination is Ignatius's way of coming to know Jesus. Knowing Jesus, so as to love him more intimately, in order to follow him more closely, is what our life is all about. For Ignatius, then, our Gospel-centered prayer to know, love, and follow Jesus is key to our growth and maturity as Christians and as Jesuits. This kind of praying is not just a retreat-time experience. Just as in every Eucharist the Gospel has an integral place, so in the daily prayer of our life the Gospel familiarity with Jesus is ever present.

Knowing Jesus also links us with the visions of Ignatius. In his *Autobiography* Ignatius describes his fourth vision— repeated a number of times and often of long duration throughout his life—of the humanity of Christ. And also of Mary, or, as he refers to her, "our Lady." Again we have a peculiar description by Ignatius: a white body, no distinction of members, but giving him great consolation. What might this kind of vision mean? The white body, of course, relates to the creation symbol from his previous vision. But the non-distinction of members seems to indicate for

33

Ignatius the acceptance of his humanity, the "wholeness" of being human—my looks, my height, my weight, my limp. For Ignatius, it is *this* very humanity that Jesus and he share. And *that* gives Ignatius great consolation.

A Call Consideration

What do we learn about God in the Call of the King consideration? We see, first of all, that the initiative comes from Christ. Christ does the calling *now*, just as he has done the calling in the Gospel passages. That is the Ignatian perspective. We observe that, theologically, we might say more correctly that the initiative is from God the Father. We see the expression of this initiative when, in the Gospel transfiguration passage, God's voice thunders out: "This is my beloved Son. Listen to him." Regardless of how we attribute the initiative back to the Trinitarian relations, the initiative is always from God (as in God's first call to us in creating us). We remain respondents to one more gift of God in Jesus—the call.

The common word we use—*call*—does not capture well the quality of the initiative taken by God or by Christ. Jesus does not issue an invitation or call in which he has no personal feeling or involvement. I believe that, because Jesus is on fire with his mission, we can rightly say "Jesus beckons." He puts his whole self into the call; his voice is strong, his eyes invite, his arm and hand reaches out and draws us in. There is a charge, like an electrical charge, proper to the way Jesus invites his followers, so the felt seriousness of his call is better caught in our word *beckons*. Jesus wants us to be with him; he wants us to labor with him. His "wanting" is what I am trying to capture in the word *beckons*. What *beckons* does not include is any sense of duress. When God beckons, despite all his loving desire, he waits. God will keep calling because he is the faithful one. But God

34

waits for our response. Our human response to God must always be willing and free.

At the same time that the Call of the King is an exercise focused on this beckoning, it is also an exercise about dreams. Ignatius couches it in terms of a story of a human king calling for a crusade. It reflects the dream that first fired Ignatius, but it is a dream that is persistent in the epics and stories in many of our human cultures. The content of the call is the stuff of which our human dreams are made.

Jesus' Dream

Jesus has a dream; it is God's dream. Jesus calls every man and woman and child to enter into that dream with him. When in our prayer we bring our life-dreams into the dream of Jesus, we find how we are to use all the talents and drives and passions that are God's gifts to us. We allow God to transform our drives and passions in ways that we could never have dreamed of.

Ignatius clearly presents to us the double aspect of the call of Christ. Jesus calls each one of us into a special relationship with him and, in and through that special relationship, to work with him for the reign of God by "being busy about the kingdom." In the Call of the King exercise, Ignatius has us reflect on our dreams, our goals, our life-desires. We need to look at our dreams in these terms: Who is Jesus for us? What place does Christ have in our life? What is our relationship with Jesus, and how does it affect our way of thinking and dreaming about life? Have we considered seriously Jesus' dream about the reign of God and his invitation to us to be together with him and labor with him? Ignatius lets us hear, in the response of the generous ones, how they want and desire to have their dreams shaped by the dream of Jesus. We are never meant to give up our dreams, but we are called to let God help shape them.

Jesus shows us, then, the face of a God who beckons.

35

We relate to a God who wants us to be with him, who wants to share with us and involve us in the work of salvation. In the Ignatian dynamic, both God and we ourselves connect with a new energy, not experienced in the Principle and Foundation exercise. We come to know a God who calls us to enter into his dreams and then waits for us, with all our own dreams, to respond.

With this foundational context, I suggest that our prayer might find its focus in the Gospel of Mark 10:17-27, the passage about the rich young man. This man seems to think that the good life, the holy life, is summed up in *doing*. "What must I do?" Jesus seems to indicate that it may be not in *doing*, but in *letting go* (as he says in the verbs *sell, give, come, follow*). Holiness is in relationship . . . with Jesus. I think that one of the saddest stories that Jesus tells is about the final judgment when he turns to a group of people boasting about how much they have done in his name, and Jesus looks at them and says, "I really never knew you." Life is about relationship.

In Mark 10:35-45, we find the story of James and John wanting a closeness to Jesus, but having some mixed motivation. From the Gospels we pick up that the apostles often argued among themselves "Who is the greatest?" Jesus does not dampen the desire of James and John for being with him, but he does point out how their eyes need to stay fixed on him, not on themselves (remember, it is a relationship!). And then they will be able to act (serve) as he acts.

A third passage might be Matthew 8:18-22 or Luke 8:57-62, which gives us a cameo of people expressing their desire to follow Jesus and then saying "but." Jesus firmly replies to them, "This relationship with me is everything. The relationship with me is your life." "Choose life," as Moses in the book of Deuteronomy says. Without a relationship with me, you are always dealing with dead things, things that are really not life-giving—so Jesus indicates.

Discipleship and Its Foundations: A Jesuit Retreat

We pray for the grace of a growing intimacy with Jesus.

The Call of Christ
Review Outline

- The Call of the King (SpEx 91-98) has long been recognized as a second foundation of the Exercises.
- The Call also serves as a "bridge" exercise between the First and Second Weeks: at once a mercy meditation and an involvement request.
- Jesus more than invites; he beckons.
- The grace we are praying for is a more intimate relationship with Jesus.
- Gospel passages for prayer:
  Mark 10:17-27, Jesus and the rich man
  Mark 10:35-45, Jesus and James and John
  Matthew 8:18-22, Jesus and his followers

Call Prayer

God our Father, on the occasion of the transfiguration, you asked us to listen to your Son. Obedient to your call, we are trying to follow your Son's lead in our lives.

We thank you for calling us into the Society that bears your Son's name. We ask pardon for the times that we have no longer listened, but went on our own way. We failed to follow. We have obscured our identity of being his companions.

Grant us now a heart renewed. Let us start afresh in listening to how Jesus is calling to us now. Increase in us our desires to live more closely with him as his companions. We ask this in his name.

37

Standards Prayer

God, our Source of Life and Goodness, create in us a heart that is wise and discerning. Send into our lives your Spirit of light and courage, and may that same Spirit find in us a resting place and home. Though the gift of your Spirit to us, may you see in us what you see in your only Son Jesus.

May we, like Jesus, profess and live out the truth of our lives: everything we have is from you, our Father. In our delight in being your sons and daughters, grant that we may find our true identity and worth. We ask this in Jesus' name.

The Standards

On the fourth day of the Second Week of the Exercises, Ignatius presents a break in the contemplative style of praying that he has introduced for our way of entering into the Gospels. The Ignatian prayer day is centered on an exercise titled the "Two Standards." The exercise, which is to be meditatively prayed twice, along with two repetition-style prayer periods, is meant to give us both a foundation and a vision.

The image of Ignatius Loyola as a military man receives reinforcement from this prayer exercise, with its reference to standards. *Standards* are flags or other symbols that give identity to a united group such as a sports team or an army corps. While it is true that Ignatius brings his own chivalric dreams into his prayer imagery as we have noted in the Call of the King exercise, I believe that Ignatius is equally influenced by the biblical imagery of the struggle between good and evil.

With a few well-chosen word strokes, Ignatius draws his own picture of Lucifer and of Christ. Lucifer—a name meaning "bearer of light"—is the leader of the dark or evil forces. Lucifer stands for all those false lights that lead us astray; Lucifer brings home to us the necessity of our being able to discern false light from true light—in other words, what allows us truly to understand.

Ignatius carefully chooses descriptive details that for him and for the people to whom he gave retreats capture the insidious power of evil. Lucifer is seated on a high throne, obscured by smoke. And the throne is placed in Babylon, a city of biblical times, famous for its pride in attempting to build a tower to heaven, resulting among the builders in the breakdown of human communication, the cacaphony arising from the myriad of human languages. We note that Lucifer is located in an earthly city, not in some ethereal outer space. Lucifer summons his minions, gives them orders to ensnare human beings (Ignatius identifies Lucifer as the "enemy of human nature," that is, the enemy of humankind [not viewed first as the enemy of God]), and then scatters them to every hamlet of the earth. Ignatius has carefully chosen descriptive details that for him and for the people whose retreats he directed capture the insidious power of evil.

Christ is pictured according to the Lucan setting of the time Jesus presents his "campaign" vision of the beatitudes. Jesus is not pictured on a height (as he is "on the mountain" in the scene described by Matthew), but rather "on the level"—designated by the Latin word *humus*, meaning the "earth" or "ground." Jesus invites us, his human followers, to go forth and try to lead all peoples to the true way of living. Obviously Ignatius draws a picture of Jesus wanting to be one with us (he calls us "friends, not "servants") and seeking our help in proclaiming the kingdom of God. It is a picture consistent in all the Gospels for Jesus calling and sending out his disciples.

The setting or context of the two leaders takes on greater importance for hearing the message of both. Just as composing ourselves in the setting or context of a prayer period is a necessary prelude for our praying, so in the Two Standards Ignatius wants the setting to be so integral to our understanding of the program of each leader that he does not leave it to our individual imaginations only, but carefully focuses the details that give necessary context to each leader and his message.

What is the program of each leader? What do they call us to do? What are the values of human living proposed by each one? Since Ignatius presumes that we enter into a retreat as a follower of Christ, he is not proposing that at this point of the retreat we are trying to make a choice between leaders. As usual, Ignatius points the direction of the prayer period by the grace we seek: to understand the *true* life proposed by Jesus and so be able to respond. This prayer period is truly a meditation-style prayer since we care called to work with our heads and so, by God's grace, come to an understanding. To show the importance he places on our understanding, Ignatius gives a unique direction: we are to meditate on the content material twice (not a repetition), and only after these two prayer periods of considering the content does he move us on to two repetitions, in which the content becomes our returning to our affect response or our insight from the previous meditation periods.

The values for human living that Lucifer demands are riches, honor, and pride. Almost being a statistician, Ignatius adds that this is the process "in most cases." In the context of the Principle and Foundation, we need immediately to divest ourselves of any judgment that riches, honor, and pride are evil. Like all of God's gifts to us, riches and honor and pride are God's *good* gifts. Riches can mean anything that makes us "rich"; our physical beauty, our athletic prowess, our intellectual abilities, our success, our power, our money. It is true that when we are rich in one or other of these ways, we receive esteem and honor from others. And then often enough we find ourselves more and more insulated and fixed on

41

ourselves. As Ignatius would have us reflect, we see our "riches" no longer as God's gift to us but as our possession, and then "honor" too is no longer a gift but an expectation and a requirement, and finally "pride" is no longer a relational gift but a solipsistic deception. Lucifer uses values that give light to our lives, seemingly giving us purpose and direction, but they become dark in the way we choose the gift as our "possession" over and against God, its true source.

Some directors may be inclined to identify the values demanded by Lucifer as "bad." But it would not be consistent with the Ignatian Principle and Foundation and the Contemplation on the Love of God. The subtlety of Lucifer requires us to pray for the grace of understanding. If Lucifer chooses good values to lead us astray, what values can Christ propose to us?

Now we come to the crucial period of praying for the grace of understanding. Christ proposes that the values for human living can be described as poverty, humiliations or powerlessness, and humility. Often enough our immediate reaction is that no one of these seems to be a good or a truly human value. Perhaps we acknowledge that these words—poverty, humiliations, and humility—are familiar to us from an older-style piety and an emotive prayer language, but in the light of calm reason they do not seem to be true human values. We need to pray for the grace of understanding if we are to be enabled to respond to Jesus' call.

As we examine the careful Ignatian structure, we note how Lucifer presents his values first, and then we hear Christ presenting his. Christ's choice of values make sense as a response to the values presented by Lucifer. As we examine Lucifer's values and the direction they lead, we come to some understanding, of Christ's choice of values and the direction they lead. While Lucifer's values are

42

good, they easily lead to a false self-identity because of our reliance on defining ourselves by the values we have chosen. What seems good in its beginnings turns us in a false direction, leading us away from true values and from God. Jesus' values keep our eyes always focused on the reality that everything is gift from God and so truly we have nothing of ourselves. We, like Jesus, are truly poor. Being poor (everything we have is gift), we are powerless and see God as the true source of our strength and esteem. The greatest gift that God has bestowed on us is shared with us by Christ in the gifting of the Spirit. It is the Spirit within us that allows us to cry out *Abba*, Father. Like Jesus who is truly meek and humble of heart, we find our truth, our humility, our value in God's gift of sharing divine life so that we are truly sons and daughters who call upon God as Father. *That* is the gift which is the foundation of our identity and value, a gift that we need to find and accept as a "given" for true human living.

Explaining the value systems that are the "standards" of Lucifer and Christ is not the same as the interior understanding that Ignatius wants us to reach through our prayer. Because our understanding of Christ's values illuminates our praying the Gospel passages of the Second Week and thereafter, Ignatius places this exercise before we begin our gospel prayer about the public life of Jesus and his call to be his followers. With the understanding we have been graced with through our praying the Standards, we will bring to our praying over Christ's words and actions a new understanding. We will see "into" the Gospel beyond the familiarity of words we have heard many times in the past.

So what is the importance of this Ignatian exercise of the Two Standards? Ignatius wants us to be able to read and pray and so enter into the Gospels with new eyes and ears. What we have seen and what we have heard from

43

past readings, study, homilies, and even our prayer now take on a new urgency. Jesus' words and actions in each of the Gospel accounts becomes fresh and inviting and no longer "just pious." We hear the "demands" of Jesus in the Gospel accounts as true invitations to us in our following of Jesus.

Ignatius has given us a way of praying the Gospels, beyond his way of contemplating. He has given us a way of "understanding."

For your prayer, you may want to consider: 1) the beatitudes—a way of truly living—as we find them in Luke 6; 2) in Luke 12, Jesus presents us with a program of how to be and act like God; and finally 3) the three parables in Luke 15, which all might be described as parables of gifts—God, like the shepherd who searches, like the woman who sweeps, like the prodigal father who runs to meet, seeks us out like well-loved gifts he has lost, and we in our turn share our God-given gifts with others.

The Standards

Review Outline

- The Standards is meant to give us both a foundation for praying the Gospels and a vision of Christ and his values.

- In the context of the 30-day retreat, the Standards provides us with two meditation periods and two repetition periods—all seeking the grace of understanding.

- Lucifer's values are good in themselves, and yet he is a deceiver, a promoter of false lights. We need to know this and use discernment.

- Jesus' choice of values is good if we understand *true* life as lived by Jesus.

44

- The grace we pray for is a more intimate relationship with Jesus, our true Life.

- Gospel passages for prayer:
    1) Luke 6:17-38
    2) Luke 12:22-34
    3) Luke 15:1-32

Standards Prayer

God, our Source of Life and Goodness, create in us a heart that is wise and discerning. Send into our lives your Spirit of light and courage, and may that same Spirit find in us a resting place and home. Though the gift of your Spirit to us, may you see in us what you see in your only Son Jesus.

May we, like Jesus, profess and live out the truth of our lives: everything we have is from you, our Father. In our delight in being your sons and daughters, grant that we may find our true identity and worth. We ask this in Jesus' name.

Eucharist Prayer

Loving Father, on the night before he died, Jesus, your Son, took bread, blessed it, broke it, and said "Take this, all of you, and eat. This is my Body." And then he took the cup filled with wine, blessed it, and said "Take this, all of you, and drink from it. This is the cup of my Blood, the Blood of the new and everlasting covenant. It will be shed for you and for all so that sins may be forgiven." And then he gave us a command, "Do this in memory of me."

Father, as we eat and drink the Body and Blood of your Son, grant that we grow more and more as the healthy cells and members of the Body of Christ. When we let Jesus bring us through the Eucharist into his saving paschal mystery, we beg that you will receive us as you receive him.

Each day, in every Eucharist, may we try to give ourselves more wholeheartedly into your hands. Help us to live this outpouring of ourselves in the missions and ministries that you entrust to us. We ask this in Jesus' name.

46

Eucharist

We remember that we are considering the Ignatian Exercises as "heart" exercises—prayer time involving our hearts. We also are noting that the Exercises have certain visions or foundations that are key for our entering into the movement and grace of an Ignatian Week.

The Third Week begins with the contemplation of the events surrounding the Last Supper. We may be inclined to consider it the obvious *first* day only insofar as it is the chronological beginning of the Passion events. But Ignatius is careful in his *pointing* of (that is, giving points for) this prayer exercise [289]. The first point presents Jesus and the apostles eating the paschal lamb meal, with all its ritual meaning. The second point dwells on Jesus washing of the disciples' feet as the summary example how we should act as Jesus has acted. The third point focuses on Jesus instituting the "sacred sacrifice of the Eucharist, to be the greatest mark of his love." Although each point is significant for our entering into the mystery, the language that Ignatius carefully chooses in this third point—"to be the greatest mark of his love"—becomes the key to our entering into all the mysteries of the passion and death of Jesus.

Let us reflect on Ignatius's first point of the contemplation. We need a certain familiarity with the paschal lamb commemoration for the Israelite people—how it is a saving event, with blood on the door lintels protecting the Israelites from God's avenging angel, with the lamb supper providing strength for their exodus journey, and their recalling the various covenants with God being sealed through the sharing of life-giving blood. We need to remember that in the covenant tradition of the Near-Eastern peoples blood is the symbol of life, not the shedding of blood as the symbol of death. For the Israelite the *life-giving* blood is sprinkled on the altar representing God and upon the people. By this sprinkling of blood, a life was being shared symbolically between God and his people. The covenant tradition helps us to follow the continuity of scriptural events involving the one we call our faithful God, a tradition which culminates in the passion and death of Jesus. St. Ignatius's first point emphasizes the continuity of the passover tradition and the celebration of the covenant ritual.

Let us consider Ignatius's second point. As we are well aware, St. John in his Gospel speaks not at all of the institution of the Eucharist at the Last Supper, but rather highlights Jesus' washing of the feet of his disciples. Jesus does the work of a slave or servant and says that he has given an example of how we are to act. The emphasis obviously is not on washing feet, but speaks rather to a singleness of attitude—service, the gift of self—towards all the activities or labors of our life. There is a giving over, a surrendering, both on the part of the one washing and on the part of the ones being washed. Jesus' question "Do you know what I have done to you?" opens up for us another reflection on the Ignatian Principle and Foundation. Jesus has given an example, a model of service. Everything the disciples have received from Jesus since their first encounter with him, they are being asked to share. So, too, in our relationship with

Jesus, we receive and learn; we too are called to share. What has the Lord done for us? What are our gifts? Do we use our gifts in a sharing way? That is the response that Jesus waits to hear from us. In the second point, Ignatius is suggesting that the work of washing feet gives us insight into understanding Jesus' greatest work, the work of redemption in his passion and death on the cross.

Let us look at Ignatius's third point. Ignatius identifies the institution of the Eucharist as "the greatest mark of his love." Eucharist helps us to understand and enter into Jesus' passion and death. The Eucharist is key to our approaching the cross. Perhaps we may be surprised that, for Ignatius, it is not Jesus' passion and death that help us to understand the Eucharist, but it is the other way around. True it is, the Eucharist shows us, even now, that Jesus holds nothing back from us in his love. He gives us all that he is—sacramentally to be the food and drink of our life with God. We have a saying that "love costs." Jesus is saying that he pays whatever the cost, holding nothing back. That is how much he loves us and loves his Father. All our scripture language about payment—ransoming us with his blood, purchasing us for a price, and so on—are all images, sometimes confusingly used (and also poorly interpreted spiritually through the ages), looking toward the notion of "love costs." God is not paying off anyone. Jesus is not buying us back from the devil. It is just the reality that "love costs."

In his *Autobiography*, Ignatius's third vision (lesson/point), after the vision of the Trinity and of creation, is the Eucharist. At the moment within the Mass when the priest is elevating the host, Ignatius, with interior eyes, saw white rays coming down from heaven meeting the elevated host, and he saw how Jesus was present in the Eucharist. Jesus is still offering himself to the Father in the gesture of raising and showing the host and still

49

offering himself to us in the rays coming down from heaven. At the Last Supper, Jesus not only gave a whole new reality to the passover meal ("this is the new covenant in my blood"), but he took it out of time and made it portable; that is, this event is not bound by time strictures. We are made present. In every Eucharist, Jesus is giving us the opportunity to be swept up into his stance of giving himself over to the Father and offering himself in love totally to his fellow men and women, his brothers and sisters.

Jesus shows us the face of God who labors, not counting the cost, to show his love. Jesus sets no limits on what he will pay; he will hand over all that he is. We human beings can even reject him, run from him, take his life, bury him. Jesus sets no limits on his love. He shares himself totally with God his Father, and he shares himself totally with us. The Eucharist is our key to all the events of the Third Week. It remains our key every time we look at the crucifix. The crucifix, seen in the light of the Eucharist, says "I love you this much. And you . . . ? In a paradoxical way, the crucifix is the symbol of the reality of the Eucharist.

Ignatius uses the word *labor* most often in the Third Week, when it seems that Jesus is not the active one, the doer, but rather Jesus is the victim, the one who suffers. But passion—what happens to Jesus—is his greatest work, a gospel paradox. Jesus' suffering and death is his greatest work—not all the miracles, not all the preaching over a three-year period. What does this say to us about our judgments concerning what is our greatest work—our studies, our teaching, our pastoring, our retreat works? Is it still ahead of us—in our old age, perhaps even in our infirmity? For myself, I no longer have a clue how to answer.

In every Eucharist we relate to a God who labors,

50

setting no limits, willing to pay whatever the costs of love—even to death on a cross. How do we relate to this God who labors and struggles so much to love us? What is the vision of Eucharist—its dailyness in our Jesuit lives—that affects our way of living and of serving?

The Last Supper ritual and especially the institution of the Eucharist are the spring-source for our entering into all the mysteries of the Third Week. Our eyes and our heart take in all the sufferings and pain that Jesus endures, but they are not stopped by these horrendous happenings. When we observe the three added points that Ignatius proposes for all the exercises of this Week, we find ourselves always seeking to be invited into the interior experiences of Jesus in every prayer exercise. The Eucharist is the key, the source, of this way of intimacy with Jesus. The Last Supper and Eucharist, mysteries though they be, allow us to enter fully into the mystery of Christ's passion and death. Eucharist is where Jesus is; Eucharist is what gives everything that happens to him purpose and meaning. We are caught up in a love that holds nothing back, a love that accepts even death—seeing death, in faith, as no limit to God's love. The Last Supper and Eucharist, then, become the spring-source for our graced response throughout the contemplations of the passion.

And so we set forth into the Third Week, where the content material is the Gospel events of Holy Thursday (from the Agony in the Garden on), Good Friday, and Holy Saturday. The prayer form, following upon the Second Week, remains contemplation, with an Ignatian addition of three extra points for each prayer exercise, so that we let Jesus lead us into his experiences of the passion. The most important grace that we seek in our identifying with Jesus at this central moment of his earthly life is the grace of compassion. Why compassion? That Jesus has died, with a lot of suffering, is history. The event has already happened and we cannot change the fact. That we can be present to Jesus in his sharing with us his passion and death is also a fact, and our desired response—the grace we pray for—is called *compassion*, a very precious gift of God to us. The temptation when we cannot do anything to change a situation is to walk away, to try to harden ourselves, to maintain an emotional distance, or to despair. In the face of these natural, understandable human responses, we all the more appreciate compassion as a difficult but priceless grace.

Compassion is first of all experienced when we *stay with* Jesus throughout the events of his passion. Ignatius is careful to point out that we will have to "work at" being present and involved in each of these prayer periods. Perhaps our familiarity with the passion story or maybe the expectation that prayer on these events will come easy for us makes the Ignatian direction all the more necessary. We may know the experience of staying with someone dear in the last hours of life; we may have been asked to be with a family member or a friend at the time of death. What is important lies not in what we say; the emphasis is on our loving presence. This is the stance of compassion.

By adding three points to the usual points of this prayer exercise, Ignatius emphasizes the importance of our moving "inside" the mysteries of the passion. Jesus is the one—the only one—who can give us entrance into his experience of the passion events. Ignatian contemplation is how we find Jesus inviting us into the most important work of his life, our redemption. It is as if Jesus were saying, "Let me tell you what it was like, what I saw, what I felt. Please don't interrupt; just stay with me and listen." As we enter into the sights and feelings of Jesus, we find our way into compassion. Each prayer period builds upon the previous one, so that compassion

52

is not just our feeling wounded. Compassion identifies the wound that is *us*, as we stay with Jesus in his suffering and death. We are touching into a whole new way of relating to Jesus.

For Ignatius, compassion in all our relationships with others and in all our ministries of whatever kind is grounded in our having experienced this intimacy with Jesus, especially in his passion and death. *Following* Jesus and *ministering with* Jesus are wonderful graces flowing from the Second Week of the Exercises. But such companioning is not enough for the true disciple of Jesus. If the presence and activity of the disciple are not stamped with the grace of *compassion*, maybe *then* one might hear the Gospel words of Jesus: "I never knew you."

The Third Week comes to a close when we are quiet and at peace while standing compassionately at the tomb of the dead Jesus. We have experienced his dying, and we have accompanied his body to the tomb. With Jesus' death, there is an emptiness, a void, a darkness, a sense of meaninglessness. Compassion enables us to stay in the loneliness. And so this new level of relationship with Jesus undergirds especially those dark, lonely, apparently defeating times in our lives. We have been graced to be with him, and now we know that Jesus is *with us*.

Once again, with the first exercise of the Third Week providing a foundational context, I would suggest that we consider Luke 22:14-34 for our prayer. Note how Jesus eagerly looks forward and wants to share this meal with his disciples. Note how, in the midst of this sacred time, the disciples can still be distracted about "who is the greatest?" Note, too, how Jesus can look at Peter, as he again overpromises all that he (Peter) can do, and Jesus saying "I am praying for you, Simon Peter, and you will be a support to your brothers and sisters."

For a second passage, we might listen to Jesus speak in John 6:32-51. Jesus is so clear and simple in saying that he wants to be the food of our life, and what that means for us. We remember that "love costs," and then ask ourselves "How do we respond to Jesus?"

For a possible third text, I suggest Luke 15:11-32, the parable of the prodigal son. Note how the father shares his gifts with his son. Note how the sons, both of them, think of themselves as "hired hands." Note how the father takes the initiative and rushes out to meet the son on the road. Note how the father throws a banquet party. We find a home and we are fed. We might ask: "Jesus, is this story about you? and us?" Let us continue to pray for the grace to grow more intimately in love with Jesus.

Eucharist

Review Outline

– The first exercise of the first day of the Third Week (SpEx 190-198) is foundational for entering into the grace of this Week.

– The third point about the institution of the Eucharist, "the greatest mark of Jesus' love," is key.

– Only Jesus can enter us into the events of his passion and death and its meaning. Compassion is our necessary response.

– The grace we pray for is a more intimate relationship with Jesus.

– Gospel passages for prayer:
  Luke 22:14-34, Jesus and the Supper and Peter
  John 6:32-51, Jesus and Bread and Life
  Luke 15:11-32, Jesus' parable of the prodigal

54

—— ⟨❦⟩ ——

Eucharist Prayer

Loving Father, on the night before he died, Jesus, your Son, took bread, blessed it, broke it, and said "Take this, all of you, and eat. This is my Body." And then he took the cup filled with wine, blessed it, and said "Take this, all of you, and drink from it. This is the cup of my Blood, the Blood of the new and everlasting covenant. It will be shed for you and for all so that sins may be forgiven." And then he gave us a command, "Do this in memory of me."

Father, as we eat and drink the Body and Blood of your Son, grant that we grow more and more as the healthy cells and members of the Body of Christ. When we let Jesus bring us through the Eucharist into his saving paschal mystery, we beg that you will receive us as you receive him.

Each day, in every Eucharist, may we try to give ourselves more wholeheartedly into your hands. Help us to live this outpouring of ourselves in the missions and ministries that you entrust to us. We ask this in Jesus' name.

Mary Prayer

Mary, Mother of God and our Mother, we ask you to pray for us that we might ponder in our hearts, just as you did, all the wonderful things that God has done for us.

We ask you this day to intercede with your Son that you might be the way that we might come to know an intimacy with Jesus that, without your help, we cannot even imagine.

Mary, keep us, like John the Beloved, in your care. Speak to Jesus how you see us so needy and poor. With you by our side, may we too magnify the Lord with all our being.

We make our prayer, Mary, through your intercession, to our Lord and Savior, Jesus Christ.

56

Mary

I want us to look at what I am calling a foundational exercise—a heart exercise—that is the first exercise of the Fourth Week.

The Fourth Week begins with a slight anomaly in that Ignatius does not identify a first day. Rather, the flow that he indicates in the last exercise of the Third Week—describing the late Good Friday burial of the dead body of Jesus, and the Holy Saturday activities of Jesus as his soul goes to the realm of the dead to announce the Gospel (sometimes called the "harrowing of hell"), and then his being raised, body and soul, at the beginning exercise of the Fourth Week—is not measurable in days. We have entered into the resurrection life, and our time measurements do not apply. And so the Fourth Week truly does not have a first day, but it does have a first exercise.

The first exercise, described as the appearance of the risen Jesus to his mother Mary, is often taken as an exercise of merely pious value because, of course, it has no scriptural foundation. Though the prayer exercise may have no foundation in the Gospels, the exercise, I believe, serves as a foundation for all the prayer exercises that follow. Inasmuch as Ignatius presents this exercise first, he intends it to be the key or source of our graced ability to enter into all the contemplations on the risen life of Jesus.

Mary as mother has had a most intimate relation with Jesus. She knew him not only in pregnancy, in birth, in nursing, and in rearing, but also in her love and support of his mission, all the way to the cross. When the risen Jesus—the whole composite of body and soul that Mary knew—appears first to his mother, she becomes the first to know the joy and consolation of a relationship with Jesus at a depth unimaginable. The risen Jesus penetrates the whole being of Mary. Mary, the first disciple of the risen One, becomes our teacher, showing us a depth of relationship with Jesus that we could never imagine— even as we have contemplated his life and ministry in the Second Week and as we have contemplated his passion and death in the Third Week. This foundational exercise points the way for us to understand how Jesus breaks through into a wholly new depth of relationship with Mary Magdalene, with Peter, with Thomas, and with all those to whom he appears, as we contemplate the various resurrection appearances. We are beyond our Second Week prayer of knowing him more intimately in order to love and follow and beyond our Third Week prayer of being compassionately present.

We note that the annunciation contemplation, identified by Ignatius as the first exercise of the first day of the Second Week, introduces us, through Mary's encounter with the archangel Gabriel, to a new unimaginable way of God-being-with-us in the incarnation of the Son of God. Here in the first contemplation of the Fourth Week we have a new "annunciation" scene. No angel this time. It is the risen Jesus. Again, through Mary, we experience a wholly new depth of God-being-with-us as Jesus, the risen Lord, presents himself to us.

Receiving gifts through the help of Mary is part and

parcel of Ignatian spirituality. Ignatius was trained at court in diplomacy. He was more an ambassador than a military man. He knew that you had to know the "right people" to get what you wanted. He used this skill in getting the Society approved and a number of times thereafter in working with the popes and the Roman offices. In prayer, Ignatius also used this gift. It is called *intercession*. The Triple Colloquy in the Exercises is an example. I believe that in addition to going to Mary and then to Jesus and then to the Father, we can also include many others, such as deceased parents, grandparents, friends, teachers, and so on, as our intercessors.

If we understand the first exercise as foundational, we realize that in this Fourth Week God is inviting us into the mystical depth of relationship that the risen Jesus represents. Locked doors and walls are no longer barriers; the risen Jesus penetrates all physical boundaries to be in relationship with us. Perhaps Ignatius is giving us a way to enter into the "not knowing," the "not recognizing," that flows through the various resurrection appearances. The risen Jesus is the same Jesus, but our relationship with him has so drastically changed that it is as if we have never really known him. Like the apostles, we fee his presence, we know that it is he, but we are afraid to name the grace of his given presence to us. This is why the grace we pray for in this Week is to let Christ help us enter into his joy and to know his consolation. When we are contemplating Mary and the risen Jesus, we are at the spring-source of experiencing the new depth of relationship that the risen Jesus continues to offer to all his followers.

The Fourth Week deals with our relationship with Jesus as he is right now. He is the One who is risen, who dies no more, who pleads for us at the right hand of the Father. Ignatius proposes that we pray for the grace to be able to participate in the joy and consolation of Jesus as he savors the victory of his risen life. Our readiness to enter into the joy of Jesus comes from building on the grace of the Third Week. Letting Jesus bring us into his joy, experiencing his consoling presence, is like turning a coin to its other face, the first face representing our letting Jesus lead us into his passion, our experiencing compassion.

We use our insight into, and experience of, the Third Week relationship with Jesus in order to enter into and experience the new relationship with Jesus in the Fourth Week. Our graced ability to experience the pain and grief of Jesus through our compassion, without being able to change anything of his history, allows us to appreciate how Jesus is present with us, consoling and strengthening, yet without changing the history that is ours. But the consoling presence of Jesus who promises a sure victory for us too is the joy of the Fourth Week that perdures into life after the Exercises retreat.

Jesus the Consoler

Ignatius's favorite word to describe the risen Jesus' ministry is *consolar* ("to console"). Jesus in his risen life is, above all, a Consoler—One who strengthens, encourages, comforts, and lightens with joy. In his risen body, Jesus represents the continuity of our human life while at the same time he shows its transfigured face. Resurrection is not a resuscitated human life, such as we see after the raising of Lazarus by Jesus in John's Gospel. Resurrection is our human life transformed. At a wholly new level, our human life is now identified with "living with God" forever. This is Jesus' experience.

Jesus knows that we live in a world that looks so much the same. It appears to be unchanged by the definitive victory of his resurrection. For example, the sun still

60

rises and sets, rains and droughts still happen, plagues and floods take place, people get born and die, wars are still fought. How do we *experience* the newness of resurrection?

Our ticket or our way in—an Ignatian strategy to grow in our knowledge and experience of the Jesus we relate to *now*, the risen Jesus—is through our contemplations of the Fourth Week. Entering into our prayer, we attempt to know how it is that this risen Jesus touches us and becomes our consoler. From the New Testament passages, we drink in the consistent pattern of Jesus' consoling role: to take away fear, to give peace, and to send forth with Good News. What Jesus does in every appearance symbolizes what we as Christians, as Jesuits, committed to his mission are also to do. Whatever our lifestyle and ministry, we in some way participate in Jesus' role of consoling, taking away fear, giving peace, and sharing the Gospel. Like the first Christians, we are experiencing how Jesus "fills" our world.

Spiritual Consolation

To enter more fully into Jesus' mission, we need to understand *consolation* as Ignatius associates it with the risen Lord. Ignatius more fully describes consolation in the context of his Rules for Discernment. Among his Rules for Discernment that are more applicable to the First Week, Ignatius describes spiritual consolation in his third rule [316]. We note that the consolation which Ignatius wants to identify as a help in our Christian living is called *spiritual*. What makes consolation spiritual? As Ignatius indicates, in its relating us to God—a gifting of the Spirit. We have times of natural consolation, times of a sense of well-being. These experiences need not be what we call spiritual or graced. We also have the "afterglow" period that follows upon the grace of spiritual

61

consolation, and this kind of period too needs to be distinguished from the spiritual consolation itself.

Spiritual consolation has its root in an experience of God relating us to himself. For example, Ignatius would say, we might describe three instances of consolation in the following way: 1) an interior movement within us, which inflames us with love of God; 2) the shedding of tears that moves to love of God; and 3) every increase of faith, hope, and charity, and every experience of interior joy which calls and attracts us to the things of God. Each time that Ignatius touches into the experience of consolation which is spiritual, he points out how the moment is always an experience that centers on God drawing us into a relationship with him. Ignatius knows from his own experience that we have times of spiritual consolation and times of spiritual desolation and also times in between, which he would identify as "times of tranquillity."

Do we more commonly live in consolation, in desolation, or in the in-between? There seems to be no set answer for us human beings. But we know that God is always working with us. The question that arises for us is: Should we pray for spiritual consolation, or is that something selfish or somehow "wrong" for us to pray for? When we consider our experience in the exercises of this Fourth Week, we understand that it is what the risen Christ wants to do for us as he did for his first followers. Jesus' abiding gift of the Spirit is meant to be a gift of consolation, bestowing strength, light, and comfort. We remember that consolation for Ignatius is 1) a free gift of God that we recognize and acknowledge—beyond our control; 2) a gift of the Spirit that creates in us a center of energy focused on God that integrates ourselves and our world; and 3) not just a lived experience, but a movement, a way to move forward, strengthening us for the steps we need to take.

62

It is true that we are an Easter people, a people in the care and comfort of the risen Lord. Our lives, our words, our actions in ministry are all the more effective the more we remain in touch with God's consoling power. This is an Ignatian understanding of the importance of consolation in our daily lives and activity.

What we learn and experience in the Third and in the Fourth Weeks is that there are new levels of intimacy that grace our life, beyond the intimacy we prayed for in the Second Week. Compassion names this new and deeper relationship with Christ in the Third Week. Consolation—Jesus' intimate action within us—identifies us with Mary insofar as we experience a relationship so embracing that it has no limits or boundaries. We have come to know that, in our following of Christ, our evangelizing activity is not enough.

The Christian disciple, the Jesuit, is a person distinguished for acting with compassion and for sharing consolation. We find ourselves in our compassion and in our consolation being twinned with Christ.

As we enter into our prayer, I suggest that we consider John 2:1-12, the marriage feast at Cana. Mary is the one who notices need. Mary is the one who gives direction. Mary is the one who shares her intimacy with her Son with us. Rest in the scene and then let your conversation, your colloquy, take you where it will.

For our second passage, we might look at Mark 3:31-35, the incident of Mary and some relatives looking for him in the midst of his preaching mission. Jesus shares with us that his intimacy is not restricted. Each one of us can be family with Jesus. We are always learning better how to be "all in the family." Mary's role is always mother. Remain with Mary, and just *be* or maybe talk.

Finally, for a third possible passage, I suggest John 19:25-30, which tells us of Jesus' gift of Mary to the care of John. Perhaps we need to talk with Mary and with John about who has been given to the care of whom. What does Jesus say to us? Remember that we are praying for the grace of a more intimate relation with Jesus.

Mary

Review Outline

- The first exercise of the Fourth Week (SpEx 218-225) is foundational for entering into the grace of this Week.

- The risen Jesus' appearance to Mary is first, not out of pious tradition, but key to understanding a whole new intimacy that Mary is the first to experience.

- Intimacy and spiritual consolation undergird our life of ministry.

- The grace we pray for is a more intimate relationship with Jesus.

- Gospel passages for prayer:
    John 2:1-12, Jesus and Mary at Cana
    Mark 3:31-35, Jesus, Mary, and the relatives
    John 19:25-30, Jesus, Mary, and John

— ❦ —

Mary Prayer

Mary, Mother of God and our Mother, we ask you to pray for us that we might ponder in our hearts, just as you did, all the wonderful things that God has done for us.

We ask you this day to intercede with your Son that you might be the way that we might come to know an intimacy with Jesus that, without your help, we cannot even imagine.

Mary, keep us, like John the Beloved, in your care. Speak to Jesus how you see us so needy and poor. With you by our side, may we too magnify the Lord with all our being.

We make our prayer, Mary, through your intercession, to our Lord and Savior, Jesus Christ.

Love Prayer

God, Father of all good gifts, we praise you for the wonders of your world. We thank you for all the ways you try to tell us of your presence and your love.

We stand in awe that you should want us and you do invite us, through your Son, Jesus Christ, to be with you and to work with you in the bringing about of your kingdom. May we drink in the strength and comfort of Jesus-with-us, our Emmanuel, as we try to offer you our lives in service.

Open our hearts to your every call. For, like Jesus, we want to say "We have come to do your will, O God." We ask this in Jesus' name.

Love

On the first day of our retreat, I mentioned that Ignatius has a number of foundation exercises, exercises that are foundational and are principles, source-like, which affect the movement of each Ignatian Week. We were considering these foundations as context affecting our relationship with Jesus. Some exercises also stand out as vision exercises. We have already seen the Principle and Foundation and the Call of the King. Now we will look at the Contemplation on the Love of God.

The Contemplation on the Love of God takes its place as the foundation for everyday life after the retreat inasmuch as it is a natural outflow from our contemplating the appearances of the risen Jesus. We are like Mary and the apostles—life goes on, but we will never be the same. We easily see now how God's love has been being communicated through all the prayer content of these Ignatian Weeks of retreat. But in light of the resurrection we appreciate the depth and extent of God's ways of loving all the more. Our prayer is that God might enable us to communicate our love in the ways and to the depth that God in Jesus does. We want, at the spring-source of our life, the grace to communicate love the way that God does.

I want to propose that *communicating* is an integral

part of Ignatian spirituality. I have to admit that being an editor of a journal has made me especially sensitive to this aspect of Ignatian spirituality.

In the final prayer period of the Exercises book, Ignatius identifies this exercise with the title "Contemplation on the Love of God." As a matter of fact, the Ignatian title tends to get us into trouble. If we translate it fully, it may say "Contemplation to Obtain the Love of God," and it makes it sound like we are meant to be busy in our prayer wooing God to love us. Or it may be translated as "Contemplation to Attain the Love of God," and again it sounds as if in our prayer we are reaching up to God to get his love. The simplest title with which I started, "The Contemplation on the Love of God," seems to work best.

Likely one of the sources for this vision piece in the Exercises is the fifth (and final) vision (lesson/point) that God taught Ignatius at Manresa as he relates in his *Autobiography*. The last vision involved no vision at all; it was an "understanding." With the eyes of understanding, Ignatius was given to understand spiritual things, he says, as well as matters of faith and profane things. Ignatius testifies that he saw into things at this time in such a way that all his studies and all his life experiences up to age 62 (when he is dictating these reflections) have never equaled this graced moment. What was so special about what God taught him? It is the clarification that Ignatius makes in naming "spiritual understanding" in distinction to "understandings of faith matters and profane matters." As we note, Ignatius did not put together matters of faith and spiritual understanding. Rather he grouped matters of faith and profane (secular) matters; he understood them in relation to each other, not in opposition. How each of them needed to be seen was in terms of spiritual understanding. This vision affected not only Ignatius's approach

68

to the world but also his approach to Jesuit formation and ministry. The Jesuit training in studies—Latin, philosophy, chemistry, economics—however profane—was not to be divorced from the spiritual. So too our ministry, whether it be biology teacher, infirmarian, cook, treasurer—no job, however secular, need divorce us from the spiritual. The danger lies here: studying theology, teaching theology, giving retreats, being pastor—all ministries dealing with matters of faith—could be exercised apart from the spiritual. This spiritual vision is what Ignatius is trying to communicate in this *Contemplatio*.

What Ignatius appears to be doing in this final prayer period of the 30-day retreat within the full Exercises is a review of how we have seen and experienced God loving throughout the previous days of the retreat—in the actual 30-day retreat, all the days of the Four Weeks. The prayer period is meant to be truly a contemplation since we can easily tell our story, we can readily call up in our imagination all our experiences of God's loving. The challenge that Ignatius is setting before us is our entering into the ways of God's loving.

How do we communicate love in all the ways that God loves, in the limitless actions of God's loving? Once again Ignatius enters us into this reflection in a deceivingly simple way. He proposes two prenotes to this prayer period. Ignatius wants us to note how love gets expressed. Ignatius notes that love expresses itself in deeds over and above words. At first we might think that Ignatius is disparaging words or verbal communication. But he goes on to describe in the second prenote that lovers share with each other whatever it is that each has. The Spanish word that Ignatius uses is *comunicar*. Lovers communicate, that is, share, with each other in the myriad of ways that speak out love. So deeds, like words, are meant to communicate.

What Ignatius stresses for us is that love is all about communicating. If there is no communicating, there is no love. We well know this from our experience of Marriage Encounter, the couple-centered Teams of our Lady, and all the efforts in family counseling and in today's programs of religious life community renewal. Communicating is essential to the way of loving, the way of being Christian, the way of being a follower of Christ. We need to remember that communicating involves listening.

And so Ignatius in the final exercise of the retreat is stressing communication and would have us tell ourselves stories about all the ways of God loving us that we have experienced—and really listen to the stories we tell to ourselves and others. Within the full 30-day Exercises, this prayer period (perhaps more than one) is like a review of all our experiences of the various Weeks. Having been reminded by Ignatius that lovers share (communicate), what do we say or do when we see how God continues to communicate his love to us?

We probably are familiar with the response which Ignatius suggests. It is a prayer original to him called the "Take and Receive." It is a lover's prayer, a prayer trying to communicate, to share what we have with God. It is hard to name what we want to share that is already not a gift of God to ourselves. Sharing gifts given is wonderful, but what, if anything, do *we* have to share with God that God does not have?

The brilliance of Ignatius's prayer is his pinpointing our "gift" to God: liberty, the potential of freedom since God invites and realizes true freedom for us. In our offering our "liberty" (our potential for freely acting) we are exercising our freedom; "our" memories, which God does not have without our sharing them; "our" understandings, crazy and limited though they may be, but God does not have them without our sharing them; "our" choices, peculiar as liking and ordering chitlins and cucumber ice cream, we can share with God. As a lover, I don't give up or give away anything. I am not asking to get Alzheimers, go crazy, and so on, which perhaps the words may sound like. "Take, Lord, and receive all my liberty, all my memory, and so on." No, as a lover, all I do is *share with* the one I love.

As the context of our prayer, to stimulate our own way of praying today, let us look at some of the ways that Ignatius recalls that God loves us. In the first point, Ignatius would have us look at all the gifts that God has given to us—the gifts of our life, our family, our friends, our religious community, our talents and education, our native country and the times in which we live, our faith, our church, the forgiveness of our sin, and the promise of life forever with God.

In the second point, Ignatius focuses us on how God is not content with just giving us gifts, but gives us himself as well in Jesus, his only Son. Jesus not only gives himself to us in his life, passion, and death, but continues to be consoler for us in his resurrected life. Jesus gifts us with his being our food and drink in the Eucharist. Jesus puts himself in our hands and allows us to be his hands and his feet and his tongue in our world. God holds nothing back in making a gift of himself to us. God works with and in and through each one of us.

In the third point, Ignatius focuses us on the effort and struggle that God continues to exercise in his love for us. God is not a distant, snap-of-the-finger miracle God. Our God is a God who labors over his creation, who labors in Jesus to be born, to be exiled, to live in an occupied country, to be an itinerant preacher, to be betrayed, to be put to death, to be raised up. It is the laboring God that we have particularly experienced in the Third Week. This is a God who labors with his

71

church, with all the differing religious belief systems in our country and in our world, somehow all working to a realization of God's reign. To see God is to see One laboring in love. Jesus even used as an image for God a woman in labor, struggling, only to find joy in bringing forth new life. I have sometimes called this Ignatian image of God a "busy God." As a result, in our own busyness, we never need to be apart from God—our "busy God" with whom we work. Our creator and redeeming God is involved in a labor of love.

In the fourth point, Ignatius wants to stress the limitless action of God's love. God has broken through even the apparently hopeless limit of death in giving back to Jesus not only his life but also gifting him with his death: Jesus wears the marks of his death forever in his risen life. So, too, for all of us, death will become only one more gift of God, restored to us in our risen life. The sun with its rays of light and heat poured forth without measure, a spring that gushes forth its waters in an inexhaustible flow are but pale images of our God pouring out his love.

It is in reviewing these various ways of seeing and experiencing God's love showered upon us that Ignatius draws up his prayer response of the "Take and receive." As ones who want to express our love, what can we communicate, how can we share, with this loving God? Ignatius gently puts forth his prayer as one way of responding, but immediately tells us to "communicate" however it seems best to us. Communicating is everything, for, after all, lovers communicate.

We can be grateful to God for Ignatius and his sharing with us his gift of communicating, helping us to seek and to find God.

Some of us might be inclined to say that since this contemplation is on the love of God, surely it is evident that this is an exercise of the heart. I am not so sure that this prayer period happens so easily to be an exercise of the heart. "Finding God in all things," often identified with this last exercise, frequently becomes more an intellectual exercise than one of the heart. We make it our objective to *understand* how we can find God in all things. The need to understand is honest, but, in distinction from the human mind, the human heart has its way of understanding, not to be expressed in words or propositions. Ignatius evidently wants this exercises for us to be an exercise of the heart. He shows it, not just by naming this vision piece a contemplation, but also by suggesting as a kind of colloquy to each of the points (the one and only time he does this in the Exercises) his original prayer "Take and receive." The prayer is an expression of a heart that has been exercised. What is love all about? It is a heartfelt prayer of surrender.

What I have tried to share with you is that Ignatius indicates that our life-vision is all important. Not only can our God be too small, but our world can be too small, and as a result our lives become too small. How do we expand our vision? Ignatius would say, "by exercising our heart."

For our prayer I suggest Luke 10:1-24, which deals with Jesus sending out the 72 disciples, receiving them back, and his prayer of thanksgiving. How do we experience Jesus sending out and receiving? What do we learn from Jesus' prayer? How does he communicate?

A second passage for prayer is Luke 10:25-37, which takes up the lawyer's question "Who is my neighbor?" Jesus' story-response expands our horizons and puts the question back to a reflection about "who are we neighbor to?" It is all about communication.

A third passage could be John 20:11-18, the story of Mary Magdalene and the risen Jesus. How is Jesus to be found in life? How to recognize him? How does he stay with and send out at the same time? Remember: the grace we seek is a more intimate loving relationship with Jesus.

Love
Review Outline

– The Contemplation on the Love of God (SpEx 230-237) is a foundational exercise at the close of the Exercises, acting much like a bookend paralleling the Principle and Foundation bookend.

– God is always communicating (the Ignatian *comunicar*, often translated by the English word *sharing*), and he looks to our response.

– Ignatius's attempt to respond is found in the prayer "Take and receive."

– The grace we pray for is greater intimacy with Jesus.

– Gospel passages for prayer:
Luke 10:1-24, Jesus, disciples, and prayer
Luke 10:25-37, Jesus and the parable of the Samaritan
John 20:11-18, Jesus and Mary Magdalene

— ❧ —

Love Prayer

God, Father of all good gifts, we praise you for the wonders of your world. We thank you for all the ways you try to tell us of your presence and your love.

We stand in awe that you should want us and you do invite us, through your Son, Jesus Christ, to be with you and to work with you in the bringing about of your kingdom. May we drink in the strength and comfort of Jesus-with-us, our Emmanuel, as we try to offer you our lives in service.

Open our hearts to your every call. For, like Jesus, we want to say "We have come to do your will, O God." We ask this in Jesus' name.

Prayer to the Sacred Heart

Jesus, Son of God and Son of Mary,
create in us a new heart,
one like your own, open to all,
ready to love, full of compassion.

Jesus, Son of God and Son of Mary,
stay with us in a world broken
but bathed in your love and your peace,
gentling our sorrow and hate.

Jesus, Son of God and Son of Mary,
send us forth with hearts on fire,
apostles formed by your word,
warmed and embraced by your care.

Jesus, Son of God and Son of Mary,
be now the heart of our hearts.

The Sacred Heart

Today I would like to look with you not at any foundations or visions given to us by Ignatius in his Exercises book. Rather I would like to make some reflections on the single grace we have been praying for throughout this retreat—the grace of a more intimate love of Jesus.

I have always been impressed by the fact that the *Spiritual Exercises* book is so free of all special devotions. Ignatius grew up in a Catholic Spanish society that certainly had its numerous pious practices and devotions, but no particular practices, whether it be praying the rosary, saying the Little Office of the Blessed Virgin, or observing a novena to Our Lady of Montserrat, are found integrated into the text and practice of the Exercises. It is true that in the history of the practice of the Exercises there have been various periods when those giving the Exercises or the adapted Ignatian retreat emphasized certain devotional practices; some retreats in the 18th century, for example, were built around Eucharistic adoration. But the book itself remains free of any particular devotional focus, and the actual practice of Ignatian retreats has been, through the centuries, consistently free of specialized devotions.

Let me clarify that, while Ignatius wrote the Exercises in a way that no particular devotional practice shows up in the text, that does not mean that retreatants cannot bring their special devotions with them into the retreat time. In a directed retreat, a director might question whether the devotions being practiced by a particular retreatant were helping or hindering the movement of the retreat. But devotions may well be an integral part of an Ignatian retreat, particularly for people with strong cultural traditions, such as Hispanics or the Polish or Filipinos.

In a similar way, the Society of Jesus has not been identified with any particular devotion, though I think that we might make one exception. Although Franciscans are identified with the Stations of the Cross, the Dominicans with the rosary, and the Redemptorists with Our Lady of Perpetual Help devotions, the Jesuits do not seem to have a devotion to call their own. Yet there is one devotion that is associated with the Society of Jesus, a devotion for which we Jesuits were known to be promoters, and that is the devotion to the Sacred Heart. Since the more modern-day version of this devotion comes from the 17th century—some 100 years after the founding of the Society of Jesus—is this devotion for us an anomaly or an aberration? Does it seem appropriate that the Jesuits should have a responsibility of promoting such a devotion when it would seem to have little to do with the founding charism—the essence of Ignatian spirituality, found in the *Spiritual Exercises*?

Let us give ourselves a little historical perspective. The roots of the devotion to Jesus through the image of *heart* go back at least to the Middle Ages, especially with the kind of mystical reflection of Gertrude the Great, Mechtild of Magdeburg, and Mechtild of Hackeborn. Julian of Norwich speaks of a vision of the heart of Jesus split in two. And Catherine of Siena experiences an exchange of hearts with Jesus. Even before these mysti-

78

cal writings, both the Dominican Thomas Aquinas and the Franciscan Bonaventure make reference to the heart of Christ in their scriptural and devotional writings. More generally, the Christians of the Middle Ages practiced a devotion to the five wounds of Jesus, especially to his pierced side, and then even more specifically to his heart. The roots of this kind of devotion are in the Gospel of John, with the soldier's lance piercing Christ's side and blood and water flowing out. It is a fact that this Gospel passage provided prolonged theological and devotional reflections in many of the patristic writings. So reflections on the pierced side of the crucified Jesus and on his wounded heart are found very early in the church tradition, continuing in spiritual reflections through the various centuries of church life.

In the 17th century we find that the devotion to the Heart of Christ is a favorite theme of Francis de Sales and Jane de Chantal. John Eudes promotes the devotion to the hearts of both Jesus and Mary. But it is the visions about the heart of Jesus, experienced by St. Margaret Mary Alacoque between 1673 and 1675, that gave the devotion to the Sacred Heart its accepted practice up to the present day. When Margaret Mary explains to Jesus that as a cloistered, uneducated nun she does not know how she could be held responsible for the spread of this devotion, Jesus tells her that he is sending her a man who is his best friend to help. As we Jesuits know from our treasury of stories, that "best friend" was the Jesuit Claude la Colombière. From this relationship stems the Jesuits' identification with the devotion to the Sacred Heart.

As we know, with the renewal of the church through Vatican II, there was a centering on the essentials of our faith and worship. Mass and the Liturgy of the Hours received the emphasis, and the many devotions that had held Catholic attention were let slide. Since even the soundness of the theology that undergirded these many devotions was at times suspect, there was a healthy cleansing of the Catholic prayer life being called for, but the down side was often the loss of passion and popular involvement by us, the Catholic faithful. The devotion to the Sacred Heart, in its graphic bleeding-heart images, in its often syrupy songs, and in its breast-beating prayers of reparation, seemed to be one of the devotions that needed a certain cleansing before they could well serve the prayer needs and devotional desires of this Vatican II church.

Father Pedro Arrupe, in a reflection towards the end of his generalate, expressed his regret that he had not done more to instill the devotion to the heart of Jesus in the contemporary Society of Jesus. Yet he was much aware that everything has its time, and that perhaps the time for such a re-emphasis was still to be in the future. I, too, do not know when or how this kind of devotion to the heart of Jesus will once again set fire to our own hearts. But, within the movement of our own retreat, I would like to make some simple reflections about why the heart-of-Christ devotion is truly integral to our Ignatian spirituality—and not just a timeworn vestige of the 17th century. Besides my own living of Ignatian spirituality, I no doubt have drunk in some reflections of Pedro Arrupe, Karl Rahner, and Teilhard de Chardin. I will not always be able to distinguish whose thought is whose since it has all become a part of me. As is probably obvious to you, I am indebted to many people, especially my fellow Jesuits (and, especially in relation to these reflections on the heart, I feel indebted to the three men I have just mentioned), for the thoughts and reflections I have been sharing throughout this retreat.

I have been emphasizing how Ignatius focuses his

Exercises on the movement of the heart. It is clear that in this retreat we have fixed on a Second Week grace, especially as I named it, "asking for the grace of an intimacy with Jesus." Intimacy involves the response of my whole person. In true intimacy, everything is shared, nothing is held back. The heart has always represented the response of the whole person. If we say that someone's heart is really not in it, we are saying that he is not giving his all. Although Ignatius himself is not using the word *heart*, the asking for the grace of intimacy looks toward the heart reality.

For me the deepest reality that is expressed in speaking of the dynamics of the Exercises is the reality of the growing and changing relationship with Jesus (God). In fact, from my viewpoint, there is a certain inadequacy or even a leading astray when we identify the Exercises' purpose or end product as spiritual freedom. There is, of course, the famous book by the recently deceased Canadian Jesuit John English entitled *Spiritual Freedom*, a classic interpretation of the Exercises in our own day. It is a most valuable book. As a matter of fact, in terms of priority, the Exercises aim at developing and deepening our relationship with Jesus (God), and in proportion to that growing relationship we have the ability to discern, and so we come to exercise a true spiritual freedom. Let me review with you how we have seen that this relationship with Jesus in its deepening and developing is the central purpose of the Exercises.

The relationship with Jesus on the cross in the first colloquy of the first exercise of the First Week sets the tone for my acceptance of Jesus as my Savior and myself as sinner and needing saving. The First Week put us in touch with everything that is essential for our Christian understanding of our relationship with God. That was why for Ignatius the First Week retreat said it all, and by his own direction was the ordinary retreat for very many people. No one of us—however long we have progressed in the spiritual life—finds that he can return to the First Week without great fruit, without experiencing anew a deeper relationship with our saving God, with Jesus as our Savior.

In the Second Week, for us who are following this Jesuit vocation and who are responding to God's drawing friendship, the call of Christ invites us both *to be with* and *to work with*, to be with Christ and to work alongside him. We hear Jesus expressing his desire for a closeness with us and his eagerness to have us work with him. The basic Christian relationship with Jesus, our Lord and Savior, is entering a new phase; an intimacy is being called for—a relationship of being a companion and fellow laborer.

In the Third Week, when Jesus desires to share with us the greatest work of his life, he gives us the key in the Eucharist—as Ignatius says, so giving us "the greatest mark of his love." Eucharist, the timeless sign of Jesus sharing himself with us, holding nothing back, speaks out the present reality of the one-time crucifixion dying. In Eucharist, Jesus so draws us into his friendship that we are being allowed to enter into his gift of love to the Father and his pouring out of love for his fellow human beings. The symbol of Jesus' being the food and drink of our life is paradoxically turned to our being taken up cell-like to be within his very Body. *That* is how we celebrate a daily Eucharist; that is why the Eucharist remains the central prayer exercise for a Jesuit community—a community which is identified with his name Jesus and whose members are calling themselves his companions.

In the Fourth Week, Mary provides for us the doorway to understand and experience the reality of Jesus' presence to us—which goes far beyond our imagining a person's presence. Just as doors and walls, space and time, no longer are barriers for the presence of the risen Jesus, so the newness of the intimacy of the risen Jesus' presence to us can only be appreciated if Mary, the one most intimate with Jesus, lets us enter into her joy of a wholly new and unimaginable experience of intimacy with the Risen One. Then all the recorded resurrection appearances in the Gospels take on new meaning in all their details. The old intimacy with Jesus may be the blinders on our eyes that keep us from recognizing his very presence with us now. Jesus rejoices to share with us the boundless intimacy of his risen life.

In the Contemplation on the Love of God, this new intimacy with the risen Jesus is what permeates the world we Christians call "the new creation." This world looks all the same, and yet it is a world alive to God's communication. Everything is not just gift; it speaks of God. God is so personally present to his world that the Eucharist—a sacramental presence—remains "the greatest mark of his love." Eucharist is a *present* reality, breaking the true barriers holding both the events of Passover and Crucifixion. God so continues to labor in bringing about the kingdom that the paschal mystery remains an ever-present reality. We live in a new creation—a creation enveloped by God, totally aglow with the light of the Son, the Christ, the Risen One. Ignatius suggests that our one response of communicating is to share all that we are and have. We want to say *this* in how we pray and in how we live; we want to say: "God, you take, you receive, we share."

Our Ignatian Contemplation brings home to us the reality that we point to when we say that someone is "all heart." God is all heart or Jesus is all heart. In our halting and limited ways, we try to express our desire to be "all heart" too in the Ignatian prayer "Take and receive."

83

Today we would say that the older traditional pictured image of the heart of Jesus would remain truer to our Ignatian prayer if the image of the heart were not to be seen in the breast of Jesus, but Jesus himself were caught up in an aureole of a luminous heart. Jesus is all heart.

It reminds me of a story that the French Jesuit Pierre Teilhard de Chardin relates about his experience, though told as if it were a third person, during the First World War. Teilhard seemingly had a wonderful mystical experience of the Sacred Heart which he recounts in an essay titled "Christ in the World of Matter" in the book *Hymn of the Universe*. Similar to Ignatius's vision of Jesus in his humanity, Teilhard, gazing at a painting of Christ offering his heart, found the defined features of Christ in the picture melting away. For Teilhard, the luminosity that was Christ enveloped gradually the whole world—yet everything still distinctly defined though caught up in Christ and in his heart. And then the eyes of Christ caught his attention. At first eyes of love like the eyes of his mother, changing then to the eyes of passion as seen in the gaze of woman enamoured, and just as quickly becoming eyes of courage as seen in the glance of an athlete in contest, and finally eyes almost glazed over and indecipherable—eyes first seeming to reflect indescribable agony and just as quickly to be alight with a superabundance of triumphant joy. As Teilhard shares, "I once caught such a glimpse in the eyes of a dying soldier as I knelt beside him." Teilhard sees with the eyes of the heart.

Somewhat as an aside, I have been intrigued by the meaning of the La Storta experience of Ignatius. Ignatius was on his way to Rome, with Faber and Lainez, when he had an extraordinary experience in a wayside chapel at La Storta. As he says in his *Autobiography*, he had been praying for some time to Mary for the grace "to be placed with her Son." Mary was Ignatius's intercessor (as in the Triple Colloquy of the Exercises) because Ignatius felt the need for a whole new depth of relationship with Jesus. He was entering Rome, having been forced to leave behind his dream of working in Jerusalem, the Holy Land. Ignatius's heart, being broken and disappointed, displayed whole new areas—like newly created areas—of a heart that can love God and be loved. The first time that Ignatius got marched out of Jerusalem on his pilgrim journey there, he saw Jesus "over" him, accompanying him, and he was consoled. Now with the dream of spending their lives broken for him and his companions, Ignatius is desiring the consolation of a new and deeper relationship with Jesus once again.

In his mystical experience, Mary is not seen or experienced; rather it is the Father who initiates the conversation with Jesus who is carrying his cross. Note that Jesus is not on the cross, but carrying it. The Father seems to say to Ignatius "I will be propitious to you in Rome." Then the Father says to Jesus, "I want you to take him to serve us." Jesus turns to Ignatius and says "We want you to serve us."

As you know, Nadal thought that this vision was meant for the whole Society, and not just Ignatius. Father Pedro Arrupe also was deeply devoted to this experience. In fact, in his last public act before the election of a new general, he celebrated a Mass at La Storta with all the members of the 33rd General Congregation. For me, the vision of Ignatius is all about heart. Jesus carrying his cross perhaps symbolizes the continuous stance of the Eucharistic Jesus in his total giving over of himself to his Father and his total giving over of himself to us, his brothers and sisters. Jesus remains in his stance of a life poured out. When Jesus says to Ignatius and to each one of us "We want you to serve us," the fact that Jesus is

85

carrying his cross and it is not the crucified Jesus is significant. Jesus is actively carrying his cross just as we are actively serving, after the manner of his Eucharistic stance. This is the Jesus we, too, have consecrated our lives to serve, and our service is the same as Jesus'—a total pouring out of our lives to God and to our fellow men and women. Each Eucharist we celebrate makes real again for us Jesuits this vision of La Storta. "We want you to serve us." It is a heartfelt response.

As we also know, Ignatius in the Constitutions (Part V) describes the time of the third probation—what we call "tertianship"—as the *schola affectus*, the school of affection, or the school of the heart [516]. After the novitiate and all the Jesuit training had been completed, Ignatius laid stress on one further "trial" (probation) for us Jesuits—do we have heart? All the training, all the degrees, all the works performed are not enough if they are not permeated through and through by our heart. Final profession in the Society of Jesus is particularly focused on the heart.

As a result I tend to see that the Sacred Heart devotion for us Jesuits was only a particular distillation of the intimacy-with-Jesus movement that permeates the Exercises. The 17th-century devotion did not seem to be imposed from the outside, but rather gave a particular and limited expression to a movement of intimacy with Jesus that the Exercises had encouraged. The particularities of this devotional practice for each one of us now need to be submitted to the usual Ignatian criteria: for us and for our ministries, what helps and how might it better be adapted and applied?

Perhaps one example of adaptation might be the notion of *reparation* which seems to be so prominent in the older tradition and prayers dealing with the Sacred Heart. As expressed, it always seems to be looking towards the past, trying to "make up" for what was not done or done badly. But *reparation*, as we Jesuits would understand it, is related to the verb *repair*. God does not throw away or start over (even though the biblical flood may seem to imply as much); God repairs. To repair something does not look just towards the past; rather it looks toward the future. When we repair something, we are not "making up" for what was not done or done badly, but rather we are looking forward to its proper functioning as a result of the repair. In the spiritual life, we work with a given situation to help shape or form it into a positive growth stance in relation to God. Reparation, then, looks towards the future, and looks toward growth. I personally tend to be turned off by the traditional language surrounding the notion of reparation and all the old ways of expressing devotion that go with it. Maybe we should link reparation and reconciliation. Reconciliation is specifically mentioned as a ministry of the Society of Jesus in the Formula of the Institute (our Jesuit Rule in distinction to our Constitutions). Reconciling as a ministry seems to be a central need today: bringing people together with their God in the neglected sacrament of confession, bringing people together with a church that has wounded and disappointed them, bringing people together in a world society of differing and divisive values. Perhaps, like reconciling, repairing is the ministry that we Jesuits are most to be about today. Reconciliation and reparation flow from people who live from their heart.

Ignatius was known as a man of devotion—not devotions. He desired that we as Jesuits would also be men of devotion. From his *Autobiography* [99] we know that he described *devotion* as the ease in finding God in all things. As we grow in our loving intimacy with Jesus, we discover that we have a greater ease in being present to

87

God in the dailyness of our life. We are always growing into being contemplatives-in-action, because such contemplatives live from the heart, being busy with a busy God.

In the context of our reflections on the heart of Christ, I would like to suggest a few Scripture passages for our prayer time. I think that we might look at John 21:15-23, which is the account of Jesus asking Peter the direct question "Do you love me?" And Peter, like most of us men, is not all that comfortable with another man asking such a direct question about loving. We might also note that Peter is all too aware that after Jesus' arrest he has claimed that he did not even know this man. How often does Jesus ask this question about our love? Is it hard to answer?

A second passage might be John 20:19-29, which deals with the appearance of Jesus on the first Easter evening and the subsequent appearance one week later, with Thomas present. Forgiveness is Jesus' first gift on Easter night—the apostles can only be caught up in it if they can receive as well as give. Remember that they all had run away, except for John. Jesus was sharing his forgiveness of them so that they too could share forgiveness. Thomas is treated by Jesus so kindly, and yet with humor. Just be present to this scene.

Finally we may also find helpful Matthew 11:25-30, which is Jesus' prayer to the Father in thanksgiving. Listen to him praying. He also promises us a yoke. Now Jesus, as a carpenter, would know about yokes. Likely he made a few of them. A yoke helped two draft animals, usually oxen, to pull together, for example, in plowing a field. Jesus' yoke that he offers will bind the two of us together so that we can be with and work with each other—Jesus and us. How do we feel about being yoked? How do we speak with Jesus about it? And, of course,

88

we still desire and pray for the grace of a more intimate relationship with Jesus—one that is "heart to heart."

The Sacred Heart

Review Outline

– The Spiritual Exercises as presented by Ignatius are free of any particular devotions.

– The Society of Jesus seems free of being identified with any special devotions—with the exception of the devotion to the Sacred Heart.

– The essence of the heart-of-Christ devotion seems to be integral to the grace of intimacy prayed for in the Exercises. The relationship with Jesus is the centerpiece of the experience of the Exercises—a movement in terms of a deepening of a relationship.

– The grace we pray for is a deepening relationship with Jesus.

– Gospel passages for prayer:
John 21:15-23, Jesus and Peter and love
John 20:19-29, Jesus and forgiveness and faith
Matthew 11:25-30, Jesus and his heart and his yoke

— ❦ —

Prayer to the Sacred Heart

Jesus, Son of God and Son of Mary,
create in us a new heart,
one like your own, open to all,
ready to love, full of compassion.

Jesus, Son of God and Son of Mary,
stay with us in a world broken
but bathed in your love and your peace,
gentling our sorrow and hate.

Jesus, Son of God and Son of Mary,
send us forth with hearts on fire,
apostles formed by your word,
warmed and embraced by your care.

Jesus, Son of God and Son of Mary,
be now the heart of our hearts.

Retreat Resources

The ideas contained in books that I have written obviously flow into the presentations made in the retreat, now in this written version. I will list three books. Yet many sources have been helpful to me and have influenced my own understanding and practice of the Ignatian retreat. I will add only two books by name here for their inspiration to me.

Fleming, David L., SJ. *Draw Me Into Your Friendship: A Literal Translation and a Contemporary Reading of the Spiritual Exercises.* St. Louis: Institute of Jesuit Sources, 1996.

———. *Like the Lightning: The Dynamics of the Ignatian Exercises.* St. Louis: Institute of Jesuit Sources, 2004.

———. *Lessons from Ignatius Loyola.* St. Louis: Review for Religious, 2005.

Campbell, Antony F., SJ. *God First Loved Us: The Challenge of Accepting Unconditional Love.* New York: Paulist Press, 2000.

Du Brul, Peter , SJ. *Ignatius: Sharing the Pilgrim Story. A Reading of the Autobiography of St. Ignatius of Loyola.* Herefordshire: Gracewing, 2003.